Kathy, You are expanding our community into uncharted territory (for us!) - We'll be to see you!

Cameron

Kathy - Don't forget us - we certainly won't forget you and the spark you added to our Birmingham community - Hope this book is a happy reminder of your time here -

Alice

Kathy -
You brought us magic and wisdom during your three years in Birmingham - It a pleasure knowing you! Send us emails when you can -
Love
Nancy

We will miss you greatly.
Frances

You will be missed in Birmingham! Ya'll come back, you hear?
Patsy

COMMUNITY
IN ALABAMA

ARCHITECTURE
FOR LIVING
TOGETHER

COMMUNITY
IN ALABAMA

ARCHITECTURE
FOR LIVING
TOGETHER

ALICE
MERIWETHER
BOWSHER

PHOTOGRAPHS BY

M. LEWIS
KENNEDY, JR

ASSISTANCE BY

ROBERT GAMBLE AND ELLEN MERTINS

ALABAMA HISTORICAL COMMISSION

PUBLISHED BY THE

ALABAMA ARCHITECTURAL FOUNDATION

MONTGOMERY, ALABAMA

ISBN 13: 978-0-615-15352-0

2 4 6 8 9 7 5 3 1

00 02 04 06 08 07 06 05 03 01

Designed by Robin McDonald

Typeset in Futura and Berkeley Oldstyle

The paper on which this book is printed meets the minimum requirements of American National Standard for Information Science-Permanence of Paper for Printed Library Materials, ANSI Z39.48-1984.

All photographs in the book are by M. Lewis Kennedy, Jr., except the following: Cathy Adams, page 3; Rhéa Williams, page 70, below; Daniel Taylor, pages 176-77; Tuscaloosa Convention & Visitors Bureau, pages 192-93.

Opening Photographs: i, Albany Historic District; ii-iii, Blount Cultural Park, Carolyn Blount Theatre; iv-v, Pepper Place Saturday Market; vi, Blount Cultural Park, Montgomery Museum of Fine Arts (1986-88, Barganier Davis Sims Architects Associated, architect; W. K. Upchurch Construction Co., Inc., contractor); vii, Newbern Volunteer Fire Department and Town Hall; x, Greene County Court-house; xi, UAB Campus Recreation Center; xii-xiii, Blount Cultural Park; xiv-1, U.S. Post Office, Mooresville, detail; 2, Rickwood Field; 3, Redmont neighborhood overlooking Birmingham city center; 4 (both), Alabama Highway 14; 5, Mt Laurel. *See index to locate additional images and information.*

CONTENTS

FOREWORD

ALABAMA ARCHITECTURE: LOOKING AT BUILDING AND PLACE was a beautiful gift to the citizens of Alabama. Alice Bowsher's articulate and insightful commentary, Lewis Kennedy's striking photographs, and Robin McDonald's splendid graphic design showed us a rich architectural heritage—both historic and contemporary—across the state. The Alabama Architectural Foundation published the book to build awareness of the value of architecture and how it affects our lives in powerful and significant ways.

Now the AAF is publishing a new book in conjunction with the American Institute of Architects' 150th anniversary in 2007. This book allows us to step back from *Alabama Architecture's* focus on individual buildings and see our built environment in a broader context. *Community in Alabama: Architecture for Living Together* showcases places that create and nurture community, reuniting the talented team of the earlier book. In this newest venture, as in the previous volume, the AAF wishes to acknowledge the Alabama Historical Commission for offering critical initial support as well as subsequent input and information.

What are the attributes of places that draw people together in community? What makes a community livable? We all know when we have experienced a place that is memorable, pleasurable, beautiful—a place that makes us want to linger. As our modern pace of life and patterns of building threaten our traditional sense of community, it is important to remember those places we value and to identify their essential characteristics.

The AIA has given us a tool for doing this—a yardstick for creating community, whether at the scale of a street or a neighborhood or a city. The yardstick is "10 Principles for Livable Communities," a part of the AIA's 150th anniversary program (illustrated at www.aia.org/livable). The principles are these:

1. Design on a human scale: compact, pedestrian-friendly communities connect people with people and people with needed activities.
2. Provide choices: diversity in housing, shopping, places to play, age groups makes more varied and lively places.

3. Encourage mixed-use development: integrate the components of day-to-day life.

4. Preserve urban centers: capture existing investment and symbolic importance in the heart of community.

5. Vary transportation options: provide good ways to walk, bike, bus—for less congestion, better health and environmental stewardship.

6. Build vibrant public spaces: create good places to be together in community.

7. Create a neighborhood identity: celebrate distinctive character.

8. Protect environmental resources: promote long-term sustainable practices in development and reinvestment.

9. Conserve landscapes: the countryside is part of our sense of place, our historic economy, our relationship to the land; once good open spaces are lost you can never get them back.

10. Design matters: good design adds value and creates a legacy for future generations.

Community in Alabama incorporates these ideas while it builds on a framework presented almost fifty years ago by Kevin Lynch. In his landmark book, Image of the City, Lynch identified five fundamental elements of place-making that shape city image: paths, edges, districts, nodes, and landmarks. He pointed out that "nothing is experienced by itself, but always in relation to its surroundings, the sequences of events leading up to it, the memory of past experiences . . . Image is soaked in memories and meanings." Community in Alabama adds to this perspective other key elements of urban and townscape design, including the seminal work of William H. Whyte.

As you page through this book, you will encounter special places that enrich our heritage and sense of who we are. The Alabama Architectural Foundation hopes that you will also have a renewed sense of why good design—creating places where we can come together—is fundamental to our quality of life. Enjoy!

—Cheryl Morgan, AIA

Gresham Professor of Architecture/Director, Auburn Urban Studio

D O N O R S

THE ALABAMA ARCHITECTURAL FOUNDATION GRATEFULLY ACKNOWLEDGES the generous support of those listed below, demonstrating their interest in and appreciation for our state and the buildings and places that make it special.

Special Gifts
The American Institute of Architects
Alabama Council of The American Institute of Architects
Birmingham Chapter of The American Institute of Architects

Foundations
Alabama Power Foundation, Birmingham
Energen–Alagasco, Birmingham
The Daniel Foundation of Alabama
The J. L. Bedsole Foundation, Mobile
The Community Foundation of Greater Birmingham
Ronne and Donald Hess Foundation, Birmingham
Sybil H. Smith Charitable Trust, Mobile
The Thompson Foundation, Birmingham
The Goodrich Family Foundation, Birmingham

Benefactors
CMH Architects, Inc., Birmingham
Davis Architects, Inc., Birmingham
Henry Brick Company, Inc., Selma

Patrons
Giattina Aycock Architecture Studio, Birmingham
R. Scott Williams, Architect, Montgomery
Birchfield Penuel & Associates LLC, Birmingham
B. L. Harbert International, LLC, Birmingham
Brasfield & Gorrie, LLC, Birmingham
Carapace, LLC, & DuPont™ Corian® Division
Gresham Smith & Partners, Birmingham
HKW Associates, PC, Birmingham
J. F. Day & Company, Birmingham
JH Partners Architecture and Interiors, Huntsville
Kahn South, Inc., Birmingham
KPS Group, Inc., Birmingham
Robins & Morton, Birmingham
SKT Architects, P.C., Huntsville

Sponsors
Brown Chambless Architects, Inc., Montgomery
ArchitectureWorks, LLP, Birmingham
Henry Sprott Long & Associates, Architects, Birmingham
Lathan Associates Architects, P.C., Birmingham
Rob Walker Architects, LLC, Birmingham
TAG/The Architects Group, Inc., Mobile
Holmes & Holmes, Architects, Mobile
Designform, Inc.–Craig & Vicki Rogers, Birmingham
Structural Design Group, Inc., Birmingham

AmSouth Bancorporation, Birmingham
Sylvia & Richard Barrow, FAIA, Birmingham
Joan & Daniel D. Bennett, FAIA, Auburn
Chapman Sisson Architects, Inc., Huntsville
Pat & Jim Conrad, Birmingham
Emack Slate Company, Inc., Birmingham
Golden & Associates Construction, LLC, Birmingham
Goodwyn, Mills & Cawood, Inc., Montgomery
Israel & Associates, P.C., Birmingham
J. R. Prewitt & Associates, Birmingham
LBYD, Inc., Birmingham
Masonry Arts, Inc., Bessemer
Neel-Schaffer, Inc., Birmingham
Stone Building Company, Inc., Birmingham
TRO Jung|Brannen, Birmingham

Associates
Herrington Architects P.C., Birmingham
Alabama Fellows of the American Institute of Architects
Northeast Alabama Chapter AIA in memory of Bill Christian, Architect, AIA, Anniston
Joseph L. Bynum, AIA, Birmingham
Dungan & Nequette Architects, Birmingham
Gallet & Associates, Inc., Birmingham
The Garrison Barrett Group, Birmingham
Nobel & Renis Jones, AIA, Montgomery
Mayer Electric Supply Company, Inc., Birmingham
Adele & Charles Moss, Jr., AIA, Birmingham
Kippy Tate, AIA, Alabama Building Commission
Williams Blackstock Architects, P.C., Birmingham

Friends
Harrell G. Gandy, AIA, Montgomery
Parker A. Narrows, AIA, Montgomery
Fuller & Thompson Architects, Inc., Birmingham
Harris & Associates, Architects/Planners LLC, Birmingham
Carl V. Kling, Jr., AIA, Mobile
Cheryl Morgan, AIA, Auburn University Urban Studio, Birmingham
William Camp, AIA, Birmingham
Bill Ingram Architect, Birmingham
Jim Waters & Associates–Architect, Birmingham
James R. Aycock, Jr., AIA, Birmingham
Patrick B. Davis, Jr., AIA, Birmingham
James C. Griffo, AIA, Birmingham
Arthur Hargrove, AIA, Huntsville
Jay W. Jenkins, AIA, Anniston
Chris Mayer, C. R. Mayer & Company, Inc., Birmingham
Jim H. Seay, Jr., AIA, Montgomery
Patricia E. Sherman, AIA, Gadsden
Larry Vinson, CAE, Executive Director, Alabama Council AIA
James L. (Butch) Wyatt, Alabama Concrete Industries Association, Montgomery
Frederick L. Yeager, AIA, Birmingham
Philip E. Black, AIA, Birmingham
Cooper & Associates, Architects, LLC, Gadsden
Susan & Roy M. Glover, Jr., AIA, Birmingham
Douglas Burtu Kearley, Architect, Inc., Mobile

P R E F A C E

IN THE MIDST OF A COLLEGE REUNION LAST SUMMER, I suddenly realized the link between my Hollins experience and this book. My college years shaped understanding and expectations of community that were so deeply ingrained I had forgotten their roots. Living on a historic red-brick-and-white-columned campus, its wide porches filled with rocking chairs and conversation, I entered into a place where living and learning intersected and mountains rose in the distance, a place of stimulating ideas and lighthearted play. Over the course of a year's study in Paris, I had the joy of discovering life in a great city full of memorable architecture and public spaces. And on a raft trip down the Mississippi, days after graduation, I found adventure with a floating community of classmates, exploring the river and towns and cities all the way from Paducah, Kentucky, to New Orleans. So, unexpectedly, I find that this book about community in Alabama has at its core lessons learned in other places decades ago: a first-hand knowledge of how architecture and the land shape people as well as places and a keen appreciation for the physical, aesthetic, and emotional dimensions of community.

To this personal understanding I would add one more insight. It comes from the Alabama Black Belt, from a saying that my 98-year-old aunt Lida, who lived most of her life in Eutaw, passed on to me years ago. It was a typical Southern quip, an observation with a touch of humor, a touch of irony, a touch of truth. "You know," she said, "why there is nobody from Greene County in Bryce Hospital*—it's because they are all down at the courthouse square in Eutaw." It is a statement about the bonds of community and how a community accepts its own, however peculiar their ways and eccentricities.

I hope my perspective on community, out of which this book has risen, resonates with readers as they make their way through its pages.

Methodology

This book started with an invitation from the Alabama Architectural Foundation to suggest places to include. More than 700 members of the Alabama Council of the American Institute of Architects and more than 100 members of the Alabama Chapter of the American Society of Landscape Architects, as well as other designers, art and architectural historians, urban designers, and historic preservationists, were invited to respond.

I looked for sites that met our underlying goal of raising awareness of how places shape community in positive ways. Each place needed to represent (with an occasional imaginative stretch) one of the eight community design elements that make up the book's chapters. Sites needed to translate into memorable images and they needed to have con-

*The large state hospital for the mentally ill in nearby Tuscaloosa

tinuing community involvement. In order to have a broader reach, I opted to exclude sites that were in the previous book, *Alabama Architecture: Looking at Building and Place.* Finally, I sought variety—visual, chronological, geographical, functional.

The result is not perfect. Despite an effort to represent the noteworthy buildings of all regions of the state, there is a disproportionate number of places from the Birmingham area, reflecting a concentration of resources in the state's leading city and my own familiarity with it. The fact that the majority of places date from the late nineteenth and twentieth centuries reflects the nature of the state's development patterns as well as the challenge of assessing the enduring quality of recently completed architecture. Of course, the choices also reflect my personal enthusiasms. Although many people contributed ideas about what to include, the decisions ultimately were mine alone.

For the captions and building credits, likewise, although numerous people generously provided information and insight, I am responsible for the final content and accuracy. This is true for the chapter introductions as well.

Sources

Sources cited in the chapter essays are listed in the Sources/Bibliography at the back of the book. All works and authors cited in the captions appear with complete publication information in the Bibliography.

Building and Site Information

The term *contractor* usually means general contractor. Years given are the dates of construction. Dates and architect/contractor credits generally relate to what is seen in the photographs; occasionally such information is provided about other major work related to the building or site, but not pictured. City and state are given only for out-of-state architects and contractors; for Alabama architects and contractors, no city is given. The current name of architectural firms and contracting companies is generally used, even though they may have been operating under a different name at the time of the project.

Initials at the end of the caption credits stand for the following designations: HABS—Historic American Buildings Survey; HAER—Historic American Engineering Record; NM—National Monument; NHL—National Historic Landmark; NHS—National Historic Site; NHT—National Historic Trail; NR—National Register of Historic Places (listed individually or as part of a National Register historic district).

Every attempt has been made to obtain complete and accurate information for the book, but inevitably corrections, additions, and/or new material will come to light. I will be pleased to receive documentation of such information.

—Alice Meriwether Bowsher

ACKNOWLEDGMENTS

MANY PEOPLE DESERVE CREDIT FOR THIS BOOK. Charles Moss had the idea to publish a sequel to *Alabama Architecture: Looking at Building and Place,* and the Alabama Architectural Foundation concurred. Photographer Lewis Kennedy and designer Robin McDonald contributed their distinct talents and creativity as I developed the concept and brought it to fruition. And once again Robert Gamble and Ellen Mertins of the Alabama Historical Commission shared their rich knowledge of the state's architecture in the process of site selection and reviewing the manuscript.

I owe special thanks to Lynda Wright, who generously gave me the benefit of her editorial skills and insights and her meticulous fact checking. Architects Cheryl Morgan, Everett Hatcher, and Patrick Davis contributed to the book on behalf of the Alabama Architectural Foundation. As with the previous book, I also drew on years of exchanges with Gray Plosser about architecture and urban design.

I am grateful to the many individuals who suggested places to include in the book and who provided valuable information and reviews for specific captions and credits. They include Bryding Adams, Ralph and Linda Allen, John and Kirk Andrews, Donald E. Armstrong, Jr., Lindy Ashwander, Malissa Bailey, Charles Barnette, Devereaux Bemis, Lola Bennett, Nancy Reynolds Bennett, Ann Boutwell, Camille Bowman, Father C. J. Boyle, Kirk Brooker, Daniel Fate Brooks, Houston Brown, Ollie Brown, John Bundy, Milly Caudle, Jim Causey, Sheila Chaffin, Lowell Christy, Jane Ellen Clark, Madelyn Coar, Penny Coleman,

Richard Compton, Pete Conroy, Fred Conway, Hester Cope, Cathy Crenshaw, Rick Davidson, Ida Davis, J. Mason Davis, Bill Deal, Debbie Deese, Eric Deloney, Melinda Dunn, Joel Eliason, Al Etheridge, Leigh Ferguson, Beth Floyd, Linda and Gene Ford, Letha Mae Foster, William Foster, Wayne Fuller, Faye Gaston, Roy Glover, Chris Green, Sara Anne Gibson, Dot Gudger, Booth Gunter, Bill Gwin, James Haas, Mrs. Ralph Hall, Shirley Hammond, Tracy Hayes, Karen Henricks, Mary S. Hoffschwelle, Bobby Holladay, Nicholas H. Holmes, Jr., Nancy Holmes, and Nicholas H. Holmes, III, Scott Howell, Richard B. Hudgens, Delos D. Hughes, George M. Ingram, Jim James, Jerry B. Jones, Norwood Kerr, Eric A. Kidwell, Joyce Lane, Helen Shores Lee, Mark Lindsay, Sara Love, Virginia Lowery, Gale Main, Willie A. Maise, Judy Manning, Lorenzo McCants, Geraldine McLain, Barbara McLaurine, Tyrone Means, Robert Mellown, Mobile Historic Development Commission, Philip A. Morris, Darlene Negrotto, Steve Norman, Michael Panhorst, Jim Parker, Della Pender, Debbie Pendleton, Jack Plunk, Will Ponder, Judy Prince, Douglas C. Purcell, Sam Rumore, Elizabeth S. Sanders, Bill Scourtes, Cynthia Shackelford, Mark Shelby, Craig Sheldon, Barbara Shores, Frances Sibley, John Sledge, Garland Cook Smith, Ronnie Smith, Katie Smith-Strickland, Richard Spraggins, Calvin Steindorff, Don A. Steen, Bill Taylor, Judy Taylor, Essie B. Thomas, Caron Thornton, Don Trowbridge, Stuart Upton, Dorothy Walker, George Walthall, Lee Walthall, Robert Walthall, Warren Weaver, Bill Wible, Janine Woods, Julian and Leon Young, and Mary Ellen Zoghby. In addition, thanks go to all the architects, landscape architects, consultants, and contractors, and their representatives, who reviewed the material to help ensure its accuracy.

I also want to acknowledge the authors of numerous National Register and Alabama Register nominations in the files of the Alabama Historical Commission and the authors of Historic American Buildings Survey (HABS) and Historic American Engineering Record (HAER) documentation available through the Library of Congress American Memory website.

CREATING COMMUNITY

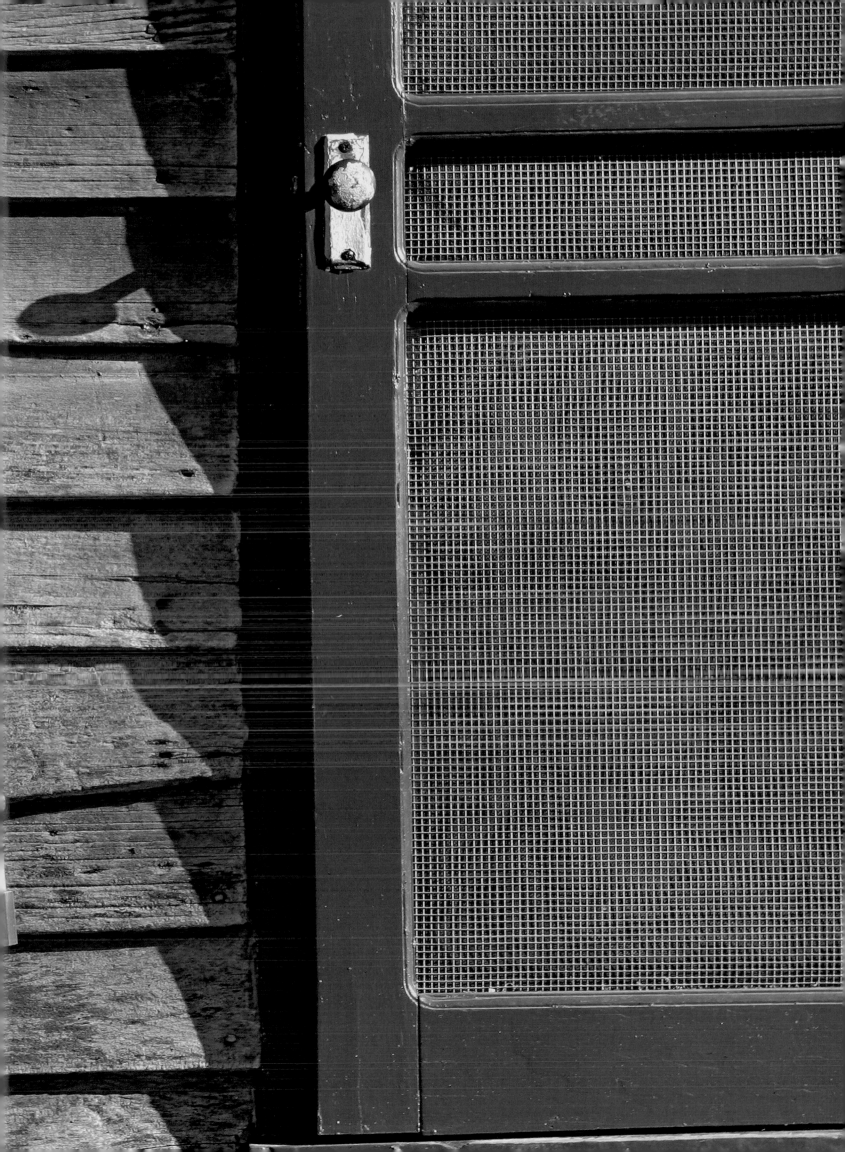

There is such a thing as a common physical place that is designed for us all to come together and that, in and of itself, symbolizes our shared sense of community.

—PAUL GOLDBERGER, *Buildings Against Cities: The Struggle to Make Places*

IN THE SOUTH, our understanding of *community* is steeped in our sense of place. The word evokes images of small towns around courthouse squares, of porches and sidewalks and neighborhood schools, of soda fountains and ball fields. It calls to mind buildings clustered at rural crossroads, and profiles of familiar landmarks on an urban skyline.

At its core, community is about people living together. It is born of our desire to connect and communicate—and to belong. Community is the place where we learn that "no man is an island," where we experience that our lives are inevitably linked together. It is where we meet the joys and the harsh realities of being human. Community is rooted in the common ground we share, as our lives unfold.

This book celebrates those shared spaces—and calls attention to the role of architecture and landscape design in creating them. It looks at how design can give a community clarity, coherence, and order, as well as beauty and delight, and at how design can help define a community's identity and values. We see this expressed in handsome places of worship standing in the heart of town, their steeples marking a congregation's hopes and aspirations. We see it in sidewalks that knit together neighborhoods and link them to the daily exchanges on Main Street. We see it in gathering places that provide for chance encounters that feed our connectedness.

To begin to understand the ways in which architecture and design help create community, we will look at eight design elements. These elements, each a chapter of the book, are *landmarks, identity, centers, paths, districts, edges and gateways, connecting fabric,* and *meaning.* Often these elements function in multiple ways to help create community. Thus a landmark may also be a center and a source of identity and meaning; a district may be characterized by its connecting fabric, distinctive paths, and edges and gateways. Focusing on key design elements is not meant to suggest that there is a simple formula for creating community character. It is intended instead to help the reader recognize some particular ways that design adds specific value to the places we live. With this approach we can begin to develop a sense of the interconnected ingredients that make up vital, viable communities. And we begin to learn how architects, landscape architects, and other designers use these ingredients to shape the way we live together.

Be aware that this book is not a primer for designing a community. Rather, as in the companion book *Alabama Architecture: Looking at Building and Place*, it aims to heighten awareness of special Alabama places and to open readers' eyes to the design concepts they represent—and to the knowledge that what we surround ourselves with matters. Of course good design

alone cannot make a healthy community. For a community to flourish also requires a supportive local economy, regulatory climate, and investment history, along with satisfaction of such basic needs as safety, education, and affordable housing.

If we value community, and if we believe that design decisions impact community quality, then we must confront our failures. For we all bear some responsibility for the nature of our surroundings. Far too often we create places to serve automobiles rather than people. We build busy highways to get us from home to work to gym to shop with little provision for walking

pleasantly from one spot to another, for chance encounters with neighbors and friends. As we have grown increasingly accustomed to life in cars, our physical connectedness to the people and places of our communities has diminished. The negative consequence of this car dependency has crept up on us. Population growth, prosperity, and materialism, along with heavily subsidized highways, have fueled a continuing cycle of more and more cars . . . leading to declines in public transportation, walking, and pedestrian-friendly settings . . . leading to more and more cars. Meanwhile we strive to compensate for what we have lost with exercise regimes and overseas travel to enjoy the street life of other cultures!

4

We are abandoning existing investment in central locations for bigger, newer (and often mediocre) developments sprawled across what was once scenic countryside. In too many places, these developments fail to create a genuine sense of connectedness—at the same time that they are sucking the life out of once-healthy town and city centers. We trade character-rich older buildings that represent our roots for bland big boxes isolated in vast expanses of asphalt. We may contend that we are getting more for less, or that what is old cannot be revitalized, or that with changing lifestyles community matters less. And yet, we continue to long for a sense of community, and to be drawn to shared experiences in places of quality and authenticity.

If we care about these things, what can we do? We can start by recognizing the value of the vital communities we have. We can celebrate places that nurture our living together. And we can ask that new development serve not only the specific market need but also the broader public need. This is a provocative challenge because it pits individual fulfillment and reward against communal cooperation. It tests our willingness to curtail personal profit and convenience for the greater good. It also requires designers and the clients who pay them—to look beyond the bounds of the specific project to relate to what is already there *and* to help shape for the better what may come in the future. This means seeing the components of communities not as isolated, discrete entities but as part of a continuum. It means finding proper balance in the tension between continuity and change. Good development will come from a partnership of the public, their elected representatives, the regulatory agencies, and the developers.

The essential message of this book is the importance of creating and sustaining people-oriented places. As you turn the pages, think about what we are doing today. Are we creating and preserving places that enrich us? Or are we eroding our sense of community? What are we expressing about ourselves? What is our legacy for the next generation?

When we serve the common good, we all benefit.

ANDMARKS

The town's water tower, built in the early nineteen-hundreds, was its civic reference point, as its several white church steeples were its spiritual ones . . . Whenever you were walking in the fields . . . you could scan the horizon for the water tower just above the tree line and know where you were.

—IAN FRAZIER, "Out of Ohio," *The New Yorker*

LANDMARKS. A landmark is a structure or form that distinctly marks a place, whether by its size or siting or aesthetic character, or by the historical memory it holds. A landmark serves as a point of reference to orient us and give us our bearings. It has an enduring quality that implies stability and permanence.

Overleaf and right: Vulcan Statue and Park, Birmingham, 1904, 1936-38. Conceived as a symbol of the city, the statue of Vulcan, Roman god of the forge, has represented Birmingham's industrial roots for more than a century—first at the St. Louis World's Fair and now as a beacon atop the mountain of iron ore that once fed city furnaces. The statue's deterioration by the late 1990s triggered a groundswell of popular support for its restoration, evidencing the icon's visual and emotional reach. Giuseppe Moretti, sculptor; Birmingham Steel and Iron Co., fabricator, 1904. Warren Knight & Davis, tower architect, 1936. Works Progress Administration (WPA), park grounds and stonework construction, 1936-38. Amaze Design, Inc., rehabilitation master plan and exhibit design, 2001-2004. Robinson Iron, statue dismantling, 1999; restoration, 2001-2003. HKW Associates, PC, architect; Office of Jack Pyburn/Architect, Inc., preservation architect; Nimrod Long & Associates, Inc., landscape architect; Brice Building Co., Inc., contractor, tower restoration and park rehabilitation, 2002-2004. NR, HAER

The U.S. Capitol in Washington, D.C., exemplifies the idea of *landmark*. Its iconic dome-topped architecture, situated atop a hill overlooking the federal city, orients us not only geographically but also politically, as a symbol of American democracy. Or consider Sloss Furnaces, a National Historic Landmark whose hulking form anchors the eastern skyline of Birmingham and proclaims the region's strong industrial heritage. Throughout Alabama, neighborhood schools, county courthouses, spire-topped churches, and soaring skyscrapers serve as landmarks, orienting us to their communities and what the communities value.

A place may also be a landmark because it encompasses a widely shared experience. It provides a point of orientation for a community's social or civic life. *New York Times* writer Herbert Muschamp expressed this when he wrote that "the essential feature of a landmark is not its design, but the place it holds in a city's memory." The Varsity, near the Georgia Tech campus in Atlanta, is such a landmark for residents and visitors who have flocked there since 1928 to relish its chili dogs, onion rings, and frosted orange drinks delivered with rapid-fire service and sass.

Over time, as communities grow and mature, they may gain new landmarks. Unfortunately, they also may lose long-standing landmarks—to neglect or demolition . . . or simply to being obscured by taller buildings. When a community loses a landmark, a point of orientation is lost. Its self-understanding is diminished. For this reason, some cities protect landmarks by regulating their alteration or demolition. Washington, D.C., also protects the view of a landmark on the city skyline—specifically the U.S. Capitol—by limiting the height of buildings around it.

A community needs LANDMARKS to provide points of reference common to everyone. What provides this focus in your community?

Founders Hall anchors the heart and history of the Athens State University campus. *This imposing structure, distinguished by a great recessed portico set off by monumental Ionic columns and flanking piers, is the oldest surviving building erected for the higher education of women in Alabama.*

Founders Hall, Athens, 1842-44. *Hiram H. Higgins, architect; James M. Brundidge, supervisor, exterior construction. Originally two stories with central Greek Revival pediment and belfry; numerous additions and alterations between 1854 and 1907 include addition of a third floor and removal of the pediment and belfry, addition of the south wing, and third floor expansion adding dormers and mansard roof. NR, HABS*

Witness to the romance of a bygone era, when the country traveled by rail, and train stations were civic monuments, Mobile's GM&O Passenger Terminal made arrival in the port city memorable. Its massive scale and architectural flair continued to mark the city even when train service was discontinued. Today, after sitting empty for many years, the century-old landmark has been adapted for offices and a transportation hub.

GM&O Building (Gulf, Mobile and Ohio Passenger Terminal), Mobile, 1907. *P. Thornton Marye, Atlanta, architect; Oliver Sellitt Co., contractor. John C. Williams Architects, L.L.C., New Orleans, renovation architect; R. P. Carbone Co., Cleveland, renovation contractor, 2000-2003.* NR, HABS

13

From the beginning, the centermost square in the seat of rural Greene County was intended for public buildings and gatherings. In the middle stands the courthouse, an 1860s rebuilding of the original courthouse, which was constructed shortly after the town was laid out in 1838. Two other antebellum structures anchor corners of the square, along with a third constructed nearly a century later. This charming ensemble of buildings, distinguished by an intimacy of scale and relationship, is rare in Alabama.

Courthouse Square, Eutaw. *Courthouse, 1868-69, George M. Figh (rebuilt burned courthouse constructed 1839-40 by John V. Crossland); Richard B. Hudgens, Inc., restoration architect, phased, 2007-. Grand Jury Building (Sheriff's Office), 1842, stuccoed 1930s. Probate Office, 1856, stuccoed and second story added 1938; renovated 2003, Fitts Architects, Inc., architect; H & H Stephens Construction, Inc., contractor. Library, 1931. NR, HABS*

Long a landmark on the bank of the Alabama River, where guests once arrived by boat, the St. James Hotel has come to life again after many years of neglect. Local government and citizens of Selma partnered with private investors to adaptively restore the antebellum hotel, which anchors historic Water Avenue. Union troops occupied the building during the Battle of Selma in the final days of the Civil War.

St. James Hotel, Selma, 1837.   *Richard B. Hudgens, Inc., adaptive restoration architect; Lovelady Construction Co., Inc., adaptive restoration contractor, 1997. NR, HABS*

Set in the southern foothills of the Appalachian Mountains, the Winston County Courthouse commands the highest point in the town of Double Springs. Its fine proportions, classical portico, and cupola-topped clock tower accentuate its prominence in this sparsely populated county. The native sandstone used in its construction and the tall water tower looming alongside tie it specifically to this place.

Winston County Courthouse, Double Springs, 1929-30. *Warren Knight & Davis, architect; Burdick Burdick & Woodruff, contractor. Center portion is the 1894 courthouse, Andrew Jackson Ingles, contractor. Additions 1950s, 1962 jail, 1980s.* NR

This complex of modern buildings at Huntsville's Marshall Space Flight Center housed the team of German and American rocket scientists who gave birth to America's space program. While they worked to win the space race to the moon, they were also transforming the cotton-oriented economy and culture of Huntsville. The flagship headquarters building, set formally atop a podium, rises unadorned except for its ribbon windows and vertical accents. Inside, the auditorium is a mid-century design classic.

Marshall Space Flight Center Main Administrative Complex, Huntsville, 1963-64. Building 4200, Wyatt C. Hedrick, Fort Worth, architect; Electronic & Missile Facilities, Inc., New York, contractor. Building 4201, Wyatt C. Hedrick, Fort Worth, architect; Pearce and Gresham, contractor. Building 4202, Hudgins, Thompson, Ball & Associates, Inc., Oklahoma City, architect; Pearce and Gresham, contractor.

20

The only public library open to blacks in Mobile between 1931 and 1961, the Davis Avenue Branch was built as an alternative to providing a separate reading room in the main library, with access to its full range of resources. The architect of the newly completed main library adapted its classicism and massing to a smaller-scale version for the branch, with handsome results. Today the building serves as a museum for the collection and preservation of African-American history.

National African-American Archives & Museum (Davis Avenue Branch, Mobile Public Library), Mobile, 1930-31. *George B. Rogers, architect; Sunberg Construction Co., contractor. Henry Inge Johnston, architect, rear addition, 1961.* NR

Designed to be seen at a distance, the Butler County Courthouse is a striking terminus to the traditional approach along Commerce Street coming from the old railroad depot. Despite alterations that have compromised the building's historical appearance, its tall dome-capped clock tower declares the continuing importance of the courthouse in the life of the community.

Butler County Courthouse, Greenville, 1903. *B. B. Smith, architect; Dobson & Bynum, contractor. Carl Herbert Lancaster, architect; Andalusia Manufacturing Co., contractor, addition to front, 1971-72. NR*

25

A touchstone of community during the Jim Crow era of racial segregation in Birmingham, the Masonic Temple stood for the finest in African-American social and professional life. It also housed civil rights efforts that helped end legal segregation. Alabama Prince Hall Masons planned the building to serve as their state headquarters, using an accomplished black architect and a successful black-owned construction company. Lawyers, doctors, dentists, and other influential members of the black community had their offices here. Social clubs, sororities and fraternities, and other organizations held meetings, parties, and formal balls in the spacious second-floor hall, ornamented with classical details and Masonic symbols. Youngsters of the period best remember ice cream sodas from the drugstore on the ground floor.

Most Worshipful Prince Hall Grand Lodge (Colored Masonic Temple), Birmingham, 1922. *Robert R. Taylor and Leo Persley, architects; Windham Brothers Construction Co., contractor.* NR, HABS

IDENTITY

Past their reflections in the big bus windows was Norwood, the residential neighborhood that was truly theirs…The bus was passing the cluster of businesses on Twelfth Avenue—a photography studio, the Norwood bakery, the little sewing and notions shop, Murray's drugstore…People loved the businesses of their community. How would she know who she was without them? They were as defining as the stack of books on her knee.

—Sena Jeter Naslund, *Four Spirits*

IDENTITY. Identity is a signature, a distinct personality. It is a person's—or a place's—unique character.

Since cities and towns identify themselves with signs, why belabor the concept? Because identity is more than a name. When a community's identity is embodied in a physical image—whether a singular structure or a memorable street scene—that image becomes a potent symbol. The Eiffel Tower instantly says "Paris," the Statue of Liberty "New York City,"

Overleaf and right: Old Monroe County Courthouse, Monroeville, 1903-1904. An iconic oval courtroom at the heart of the Monroe County Courthouse incarnates the identity of a small town. It inspired the climactic courtroom scene made famous round the world by the book and subsequent movie To Kill a Mockingbird. *Each May Monroeville citizens rekindle all that the courtroom represents as they dramatize the story in its original setting. Andrew J. Bryan, New Orleans, architect; M. T. Lewman & Co., Louisville, contractor. Holmes & Holmes, Architects, restoration architect, 1986-2000. NR*

30

and the French Quarter "New Orleans." Such a symbol can be emotional as well as visual. It often carries associations or personal experiences tied to the place, experiences that may be infused with its particular history, geography, and traditions. So the identity of a place not only tells us *where* we are but in some ways also expresses *who* we are.

When we share the identity of a place with others, it strengthens our sense of connectedness and belonging. Think of how a local team's winning streak draws us together, or of the surprising sense of connection when we meet a stranger from "home" in a distant land. Some urban designers and town planners who value the benefits of strong community identity urge that design for new construction, especially that of a public nature, incorporate references to a place's shared associations and collective experience. This builds in continuity and strengthens a community's sense of itself. Inside the Birmingham International Airport a commissioned sculpture by Larry Kirkland, "Birmingham Beacons," celebrates the area's history and culture. In Union Springs, the Bird Dog Field Trial Monument by Bob Wehle reminds residents and visitors of Bullock County's hunting heritage and the field trials for which the area is so well known.

Buildings and landscapes that express community identity may also be landmarks, providing their communities points of reference. Likewise, identity is closely connected with meaning—that which holds particular meaning in a place also expresses its identity.

A place that expresses a community's IDENTITY is a symbol of its collective self. What place best expresses the identity of your community?

When Tuskegee students made and laid the bricks that shaped the architecture of the early campus, they were defining themselves as well as the institute they built. Their work reflected Booker T. Washington's deep-seated commitment to education, self-reliance, and community service. George Washington Carver further enriched the identity of this place as he helped transform the agricultural economy of the South during his forty-seven years here.

Tuskegee University (Tuskegee Normal and Industrial Institute, Tuskegee Institute) Historic Campus, Tuskegee. *White Hall (page 31, above), 1908-1909, Robert R. Taylor, architect; clock tower, 1913; renovation 2002-2003, Brown Chambless Architects, Inc., architect; Centex Construction, Plantation, Florida, contractor. Douglass Hall, 1902-1904, Robert R. Taylor, architect; facade modified. Tompkins Hall (Tompkins Dining Hall), 1903-10, James M. Golucke, Atlanta, architect; renovation 1988-89, Marion L. Fowlkes Architect, Nashville, architect; Montgomery Construction, contractor. Not pictured: Carnegie Hall (Carnegie Library), 1901-1902, Robert R. Taylor, architect. NHL, NHS, NR*

An expression of pride when it was constructed in the late 1850s, the Lowndes County Courthouse spoke of a refined taste for Greek Revival classicism in the midst of Black Belt farmland. Pride soon mixed with turbulence when secessionists held heated meetings at the courthouse in 1860. Turbulence struck again in 1965, when juries acquitted two men, one who killed Episcopal seminarian and civil rights worker Jonathan Daniels and a Klansman accused of slaying Detroit civil rights worker Viola Liuzzo. The grand raised portico with fluted Doric columns is a recreation of the original, which was removed in the early twentieth century.

Lowndes County Courthouse, Hayneville, 1855-58. *Raised portico and stairs removed, cupola and north-south wings added, 1905-1906. Restoration of raised portico and rear addition, Parsons Wible Brummal Alkire/Architects, Inc., architect; Richard Compton General Contractor, contractor, 1981-83. NR, HABS*

35

From its prominent perch on Gunter Avenue, a handsome marble-clad, cupola-topped post office represents its city well. In many cities and towns, post offices enrich their communities with buildings of quality that provide a central hub where citizens regularly encounter one another. Inside the Guntersville Post Office, a mural recalls the coming of the Spanish when the region was inhabited by Native Americans. Such New Deal-sponsored works of art in Alabama government buildings in the 1930s and 40s often incorporated references to local history and cultural identity.

U.S. Post Office, Guntersville, 1940-41. *Louis A. Simon, Supervising Architect of the Federal Works Agency, architect; Ray M. Lee Construction Co., Atlanta, contractor. Charles Russell Hardman, mural artist, 1947.*

Trowbridge's has been a Florence institution since 1918. *The ice cream shop, known for its sodas, sundaes, and signature orange-pineapple ice cream, is in its third generation of family ownership. Paul Trowbridge moved to the city after passing through on his way from Texas to a dairy convention in North Carolina. He constructed this building to house his milk processing operation and creamery, with his family living upstairs. The vintage interior dates from the late 1940s.*

Trowbridge's, Florence, 1918. NR

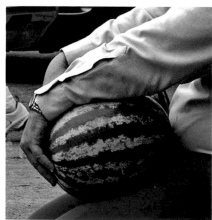

For generations, folk from all walks of life have formed lasting relationships at the Montgomery Curb Market. Week after week, and season after season, they come together over fresh produce and homemade baked and canned goods—to buy and sell, to swap cooking tips, and simply to chat. The utilitarian building with its sides open to the outdoors provides an unpretentious setting where familiarity fosters a shared identity, shaped around the satisfaction of basic needs.

Montgomery Curb Market, Montgomery, 1946

The place you remember, driving through Goodwater, is the two-story building at the only traffic light in Coosa County. It stands

on a rise by the railroad tracks, where trains still sound their whistles as they roar by. Though Goodwater has declined in recent

decades, since U.S. 280 moved several miles to the west, cattle farmers, gardeners, and hunters keep the feed and seed store in

business. And it can get crowded on Thursday and Friday afternoons, when longtime county residents gather in the store's mismatched

rockers to pass on tidbits of news and opinion and to shoot the breeze.

Goodwater Feed & Hardware (Franklin's Feed and Seed), Coosa County, late 1800s

In the hinterland of south Alabama, Malbis Memorial Church tells of the Greek Orthodox community that built it. Its impressive form rises unexpectedly in the flat Baldwin County landscape, barely hinting at the breathtaking light and color of the soaring interior. The Byzantine church is a memorial to the community's founder, Jason Malbis, who bought land here in 1906. The communal agricultural venture he began for fellow-Greek immigrants eventually grew to some 12,000 acres incorporated under the name Malbis Plantation.

Malbis Memorial Church, Baldwin County, 1960-64. Frederick C. Woods & Associates, architect; Botter and Dutton Construction Co., contractor; Spyros Tziousvaras, Athens, iconographer; Tonelli Studios, Chicago, mosaics.

*A **community of the faithful** has gathered in this spot for more than 150 years. The open-sided wood tabernacle—with pegged hand-hewn beams, well-worn pews, and fresh wood shavings sprinkled on the ground every spring—carries on the tradition of nineteenth-century camp meetings. The tabernacle and campground come alive every July on homecoming Sunday, when revival services continue through Wednesday evening and there is dinner on the grounds. There is also Gospel singing on first -Saturday nights from March through October.*

Little Texas Methodist Tabernacle and Campground, Macon County, mid-nineteenth century. *Commissary reconstructed 1998.*

CENTERS

Every good city has a center.

—STROUD WATSON, quoted in *Making Places Special:
Stories of Real Places Made Better by Planning*

CENTERS. The center is the core. It is the pivot point around which things revolve, a place of concentrated activity. For a community, the center is a place where people come together, where paths converge.

Our need for centers—for central places of social interaction—is deeply ingrained. Humankind began to seek centers long ago, when early nomadic people periodically returned to caves and sacred places. By classical times, the Greeks had

Overleaf and below: UAB Campus Recreation Center, Birmingham, 2002-2005. A dynamic design creates a new hub as it helps reshape the campus at the University of Alabama at Birmingham. The recreation center anchors the edge of a new campus green, strengthening UAB's residential and pedestrian character and linking the urban campus's undergraduate and medical-research sectors. A sweeping track that bursts from the façade as it circles interior courts gives walkers and runners panoramic views of the community beyond. Expanses of glass allow those inside to connect visually with passing street life, and invite those outside to join the activity and interaction within. Cannon Design, St. Louis, design architect; Williams Blackstock Architects, P.C., architect of record; B. L. Harbert International, LLC, design-build contractor.

developed the agora as the central outdoor place where citizens carried on political, social, and economic exchanges. In Roman cities the forum became that principal civic space, serving much the same purpose as the agora. By the Middle Ages and continuing through the Renaissance in Europe, market squares and plazas of growing sophistication defined the hearts of cities and towns.

A classic example of this is the Piazza San Marco in Venice. It is a vast open space, enclosed on three sides by arcaded public buildings and anchored by St. Mark's Basilica and the soaring belltower. Because of its central location, its public and religious functions, its grand presence, and its busy cafés, it is full of life, fed by a steady flow of pedestrians coming from paths to the north and from the piazzetta that connects to the Grand Canal. Piazza San Marco exudes the vitality that architecture critic Paul Goldberger had in mind when he said that "we must be making the kind of public space that really gets used, not the kind of public space that is put there only to set off and glorify the building behind it." Goldberger challenges us to have civic places that draw us together and make us want to linger.

Centers of community are not limited to plazas and town squares. Any place that brings people together to meet and to share common experiences, to see and be seen, serves as a center. Churches, theaters, libraries, ball fields—even intersections where people congregate and interact—can fill the role. Healthy communities have a variety of centers, major and minor, touching different aspects of our common life.

A community needs CENTERS that encourage citizens to come together and connect. What are the centers in your community?

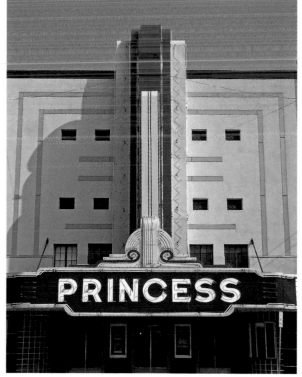

For thousands of years, Native Americans came to this northeast Alabama cave that sheltered them from the north wind and admitted the morning sun. Streams flowed nearby, game was abundant, and not far away was the Tennessee River. Artifacts indicate occupancy by small family groups and later by transient hunting and trading parties. Russell Cave is one of the most important archeological sites in the Southeast United States, with evidence that each of the four primary prehistoric cultures spent significant time here. (Mannequins at right are part of a National Park Service display.)

Russell Cave National Monument, Jackson County, intermittent habitation ca. 7,000 BC-ca. AD 1600. NM, NR

Architect Frank Lockwood designed the library at Huntingdon College to draw students with its beauty as well as its books. He distinguished the building with a signature tracery window and a soaring interior space articulated by hammerbeam trusses. The building enriches the Gothic character of the campus and reflects the library's central role in an academic community.

Houghton Memorial Library, Huntingdon College, Montgomery, 1929-30. *Frank Lockwood, architect; A. C. Samford Construction Co., contractor.* NR

An arcaded cloister *defines the historic core of Spring Hill College. Rhythmic arches unify the buildings and chapel that surround the central courtyard, providing a sheltered passage as well as a graceful sense of enclosure. Spring Hill is Alabama's oldest institution of higher learning.*

Spring Hill College Quadrangle, Mobile. *Administration (Main) Building, 1860, James Freret, New Orleans, architect; Charles Fricke, contractor-builder. Nan Altmayer Place (Moore Hall, Infirmary), 1866; east wing addition, 2005-2006, TAG/The Architects Group, Inc., architect; Doster Construction Co., Inc., contractor. Administration Building-North (Refectory), 1885. St. Joseph's Chapel and parapeted gallery around the courtyard, 1909-10, Downey and Denham, architect; Jett Brothers, contractor; chapel restoration, 2003-2004, John C. Williams Architects, L.L.C., New Orleans, architect; Doster Construction Co., Inc., contractor. NR, HABS*

57

When Decatur's Princess Theatre converted from vaudeville to film, it signaled new vitality with an Art Deco-influenced facelift and a brilliant neon-lit marquee. The Princess remained a center for community entertainment for several decades before it fell into decline in the 1970s. Fortunately, citizens saw the potential of the theater to be a catalyst for downtown revitalization, prompting the city to buy and renovate it to serve as a performing arts center. The theater's rebirth has helped spur interest and investment in surrounding buildings, including the theater's own expansion.

Princess Theatre, Decatur, 1940-41. Albert Frahn, architect; W. S. Reeves and Son, contractor, 1940-41 remodeling of theater (converted in 1919 from 1887 livery stable). Aycock-Neville and Associates, renovation architect; J. E. Johnson Co., renovation contractor, 1982-83. Marion L. Fowlkes Architect, Nashville, architect; R. C. Mathews Contractor, Nashville, construction manager; Baggette Construction, Inc., contractor, façade and marquee restoration, new stage house, and expansion into adjacent historic building, 1999-2001. NR

KIMS SCHOOL OF DANCE
JUNE 17

Fans still find community in the embrace of Rickwood Field, where baseball lives on in exhibition games at America's oldest remaining ballpark. Rickwood was an urban phenomenon in the heyday of baseball's popularity, drawing thousands of fans from all parts of the city together to enjoy themselves. The scale and intimacy of the grandstand encouraged social interaction as the crowds cheered for Birmingham's hometown teams, the Barons and the Black Barons.

Rickwood Field, Birmingham, 1910. *Southeastern Engineering Co., plans, engineering, and construction. Denham, Van Keuren & Denham, architect, 1920s additions. Paul Wright & Co., Engineers, design and construction, 1920s additions and 1928 stadium entrance. NR, HABS*

Considered cutting-edge when it was built, *Garrett Coliseum uses massive braced arches to hold up a concrete roof, creating a huge open space with no interior supports. The bold solution gives all seats excellent views. Over the years, the versatile facility has brought people from near and far to attend its rodeos, conventions, trade shows, sports events, musical performances, and horse and cattle shows and sales. The inaugural event, held in 1951 before the roof was installed, featured country music greats Hank Williams, Hank Snow, and the Carter Sisters.*

Garrett Coliseum (Alabama Agricultural Center), Montgomery, 1949-51, 1952-53. *Sherlock, Smith & Adams, Inc., architect; J. A. Jones Construction Co., phase I contractor, 1949-51; Butler & Cobbs, phase II contractor, 1952-53.*

The undisputed centerpiece of rural Clay County sits in a classic courthouse square dominating the modest commercial buildings that surround it. A statue of Justice atop the impressive Beaux Arts style structure declares the building's purpose. Below, a bell and clock give order to the county seat's daily life. Inside is the courtroom where county native Hugo Black first practiced law, years before becoming a U.S. Senator and then Associate Justice of the United States Supreme Court.

Clay County Courthouse, Ashland, 1906. *Charles W. Carlton, architect; Harper & Barnes, Cleveland, Tennessee, contractor. TurnerBatson Architects, PC, architect; US Commercial Contracting, Inc., contractor, restoration of windows and courtroom, 2002, 2003-2004. NR*

A central plot of land held in common for the entire community, the Demopolis public square is one of Alabama's oldest, dating from an 1819 plan. In 1895 the addition of a large cast-iron fountain and pool helped transform the square into the inviting spot it is today. Commercial and public buildings face the square on four sides, while at its northwest corner a Confederate monument (not pictured) stands guard in the intersection.

Public Square, Demopolis, 1819. *Fountain, 1895, cast by J. L. Mott Iron Works, Trenton, New Jersey; restored by Robinson Iron, 1995.* NR

68

Newbern straddles Highway 61, *rising out of a rolling prairie of pastureland and catfish ponds. Although abandoned stores and barns and a long-closed bank tell of the Black Belt community's decline, there is new life in the center of town. Architectural students from Auburn's Rural Studio work in a rusted metal barn next to the post office and general store, and do woodworking in the vacant structure across the street. In 2005 they added a civic presence to this cluster of buildings—a volunteer fire station that doubles as a town hall and community gathering spot. The design is rooted in the place's existing forms and needs, yet the boldness and sophistication of the building—a steel-and-wood structure clad in cedar and translucent polycarbonate—point toward the future.*

Town Center, Newbern. *Newbern Volunteer Fire Department and Town Hall, Will C. Brothers, Elizabeth Ellington, Matthew T. Finley, and Leia W. Price, designers and builders; Andrew Freear and Richard Hudgens, Auburn University architectural faculty advisors, 2004-2005.*

70

A vision of bringing people together sparked the idea of SawWorks Studio. ArchitectureWorks, the planning and design firm that

owns the building next to its offices, makes it available for uses that build and benefit community. Examples include an art project

designed to bring together students from different backgrounds and a program sponsored by Impact Alabama for Birmingham public

high school students to gain skills and knowledge through debate. The sensitively adapted industrial space, whose large windows

fill it with light and views onto a central courtyard, serves a variety of cultural, leadership, and educational groups.

SawWorks Studio (Southern Stave Saw & Machine Company, Birmingham Saw Works), Birmingham, 1924. Inglenook Construction

Co., contractor. ArchitectureWorks, LLP, renovation architect; Rives Construction Co., Inc., renovation contractor, 1999.

71

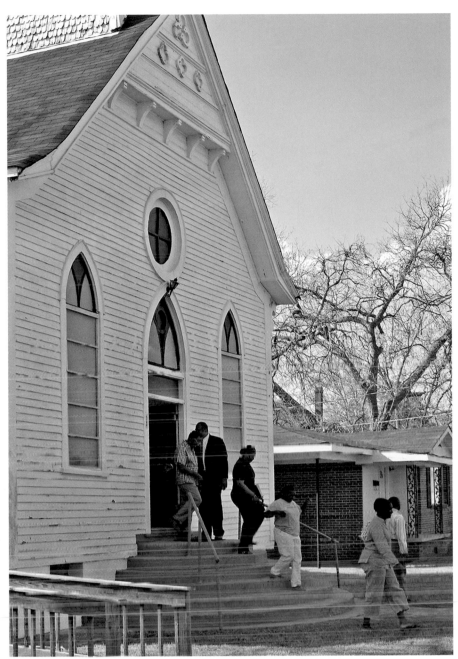

Freed slaves started a new church in Union Springs shortly after the Civil War ended. Just fifteen years later the congregation built this richly textured Victorian structure with Gothic windows and a decorative central gable and steeple. Wayman Chapel A.M.E. Church still serves as a center of worship and community well over a century later.

Wayman Chapel A.M.E. Church, Union Springs, 1882

73

PATHS

> *"The street is the river of life...the place where we come together..."*
>
> —WILLIAM H. WHYTE, *City: Rediscovering the Center*

PATHS. A path is a route from one point to another. In a community, a path is usually a street, but it could also be a bridge or a trail or a waterway.

Paths function as the spines and arteries around which communities take shape. They help structure coherence and connectedness, linking destinations and creating centers where

they converge. Paths animate communities, as we move along them through space and experience. At their best, paths enrich daily life with chance encounters and visual pleasures, with sequences of anticipation and arrival as we approach a destination.

This is why so many urban designers and critics exalt the importance of the primary path, the street. William H. Whyte, a

Mountain Brook Walkways (overleaf) and Homewood Shades Creek Greenway (above right). Walkers, joggers, and strolling parents with young children enjoy systems of trails and sidewalks in the adjoining municipalities of Mountain Brook and Homewood. The pathways encourage pedestrian activity and the chance encounters that enhance community life. A combination of new and existing amenities, they link neighborhoods to commercial villages, make natural areas accessible, and connect to schools, shopping centers, and medical facilities. Mountain Brook Walkways, phased, 1995–, Nimrod Long and Associates, Inc., landscape architect; Walker Patton Co., Inc., Milton Construction Co., Inc., contractors. Homewood Shades Creek Greenway, phased, 2000–, Ross Land Design, P.C., landscape architect; Walker Patton Co., Inc., contractor.

keen observer of how cities function, called the street "the river of life . . . where we come together." Architecture critic Paul Goldberger called it "supreme," saying it is "the fundamental building-block of the urban environment." Urban designer Jonathan Barnett said that the street is "the basic organizing principle for the livable community." He urged that "buildings . . . be designed to relate to and reinforce the street."

Unfortunately, in recent times these paths have too often become inhospitable, overcome by traffic and rendered sterile by lifeless stretches of surface parking, windowless walls, and empty buildings. How much better our communities are served when paths engage us with sidewalks, attractive facades, and interesting activities and views along the way, when paths are defined and visually unified by buildings and street trees and planted medians. Well-designed paths nurture street life, which in turn attracts visitors and shoppers and strollers, whose presence adds security and vitality. The Champs Élysées in Paris, New York City's Brooklyn Bridge, and the St. Charles Avenue Streetcar Line in New Orleans are models of how paths shape and enliven cities.

A community needs attractive and interesting PATHS to knit it together physically and socially and to provide access to its important gathering places. What paths contribute to the vitality of your community?

Prattville's main street follows Autauga Creek, *whose abundant water power led Daniel Pratt to locate a cotton gin manufactory here in the 1830s. The town took shape in relation to the creek and dam and associated industries, similar to the New Hampshire mill village where Pratt was born. The Daniel Pratt Cotton Gin Factory, which in antebellum times anchored the state's most important industrial complex, still provides the town's distinctive focus and character, looming at the head of West Main Street.*

West Main Street, Prattville. *Continental Eagle Corporation (Continental Gin Company, Daniel Pratt Gin Company) complex, ca. 1848, ca. 1852, 1854, 1898, 1912, 1962.* NR, HAER, HABS

Designed for pedestrians as well as cars, Bibb Graves Bridge provides side-walks and benches as amenities for walkers as they cross from one side of town to the other. Graceful concrete arches carry this path across the Coosa River at Wetumpka.

Bibb Graves Bridge, Wetumpka, 1929-31. H. H. Houk, Alabama Highway Dept. bridge engineer; possibly B. B. Smith, contractor.

Picket fences and moss-draped oaks
lend charm to a public walkway that
for more than a century has connected
a community of cottages overlooking
Mobile Bay. This rare instance of public
access through private land has also
provided those who stroll it a connection
to the past, through glimpses of a bay-
front landscape and way of life that
changed little over many decades—until
Hurricane Katrina. The ravaging storm
damaged roofs and porches and wrecked
the walk with an onslaught of water,
sand, and debris.

Public Walkway, Point Clear. NR

An antebellum canal is the spine of a park in the heart of Huntsville. *Originally built to transport cotton to the Tennessee River, the reconstructed waterway provides an appealing feature in a park that the public has enjoyed for more than 150 years. The same spring that gave birth to the city and long supplied its water feeds the canal.*

Big Spring International Park, Huntsville. *LDR International, Inc., landscape architect; Chorba Contracting Corp., contractor, 1995 modifications.*

Seventy feet above a deep, wooded gorge, the Horton Mill Covered Bridge has connected inhab-itants in mountainous Blount County since the 1930s, when it replaced an earlier bridge. The Town lattice-truss structure uses traditional methods and materials to create a remarkable composition in wood, worn smooth over time. It spans the Calvert Prong of the Little Warrior River.

Horton Mill Covered Bridge, Blount County, 1934-35. *Zelmer C. Tidwell, foreman, Blount County bridge crew, builder. Gilbreath, Foster & Brooks, Inc., restoration engineer; R. L. Moss Construction, Inc., restoration contractor, 1974. NR, HAER*

Designed to fit into the ambience of downtown *as well as to facilitate getting to destinations, Mobile's wayfinding sign system invites visitors to explore the city. It serves residents as well, by heightening awareness of local attractions that contribute to community character and vitality.*

Wayfinding System, Mobile, ongoing installation 1999–. *KPS Group, Inc., planner and architect; The Douglas|Group, environmental graphics design; Volkert & Associates, Inc., consulting engineer; Advantage Sign Co., LLC, Image Design, Inc., Allied Signs, construction contractors.*

Bienville
Square

Federal
Courthouse   →

De Tonti   →
Square District

Dauphin St.   ↑
District

Cathedral   ↑
Square

90

Public sculpture adds interest *to a landscaped parkway, enticing us to get out of the car and stroll. Historic nineteenth and twentieth-century commercial buildings give the street further definition and unity as well as adding eye-catching details for pedestrian pleasure. East Broad is one of several picturesque parkways in Eufaula that date from its early days as a riverboat town on the Chattahoochee River.*

East Broad Street, Eufaula. *Old U.S. Post Office (upper left; now offices of Blondheim & Mixon, Inc.), 1911-12, James Knox Taylor, Supervising Architect of the U.S. Treasury, architect; George Becking, Chattanooga, contractor. Blondheim & Mixon, Inc., renovation architect; Oliver Turner, renovation contractor, 1991. NR*

Connecting people and communities along the way, *the Chief Ladiga Trail follows an abandoned railroad bed through Calhoun and Cleburne counties. At the eastern end are views of beautiful mountains and undeveloped land. As the trail moves west and south toward Anniston, bikers, joggers, and walkers animate the countryside, campus, and small towns through which it slices. The trail is named for an early nineteenth-century Creek leader.*

Chief Ladiga Trail, Calhoun and Cleburne Counties, phased, 1996–. *Goodwyn, Mills & Cawood, Inc., engineer; APAC Southeast Inc., contractor. Jenkins Munroe Jenkins Architecture, architect; Logan Construction, contractor, Jacksonville State University segment.*

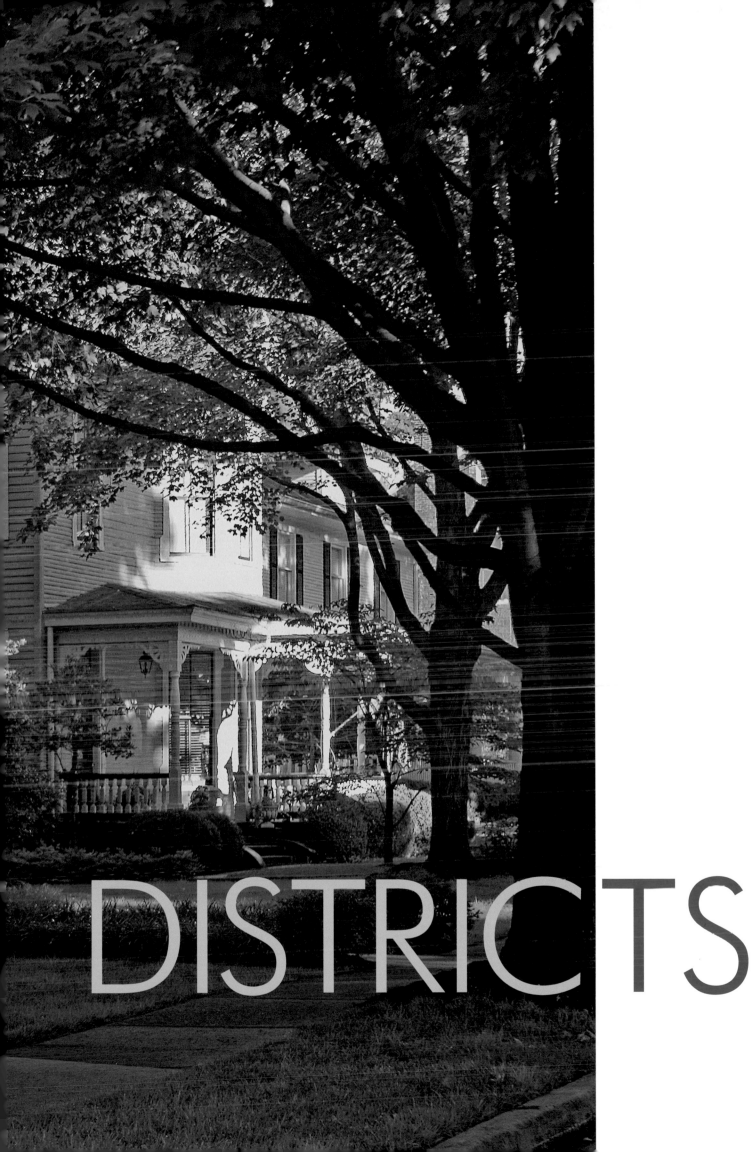

DISTRICTS

While few areas in the United States can be compared for quality and harmony to the Place des Vosges, the Place Vendôme or the Place de la Concorde in Paris, there are many in which buildings dignify a community because of their pleasing relationship to one another. In Louisburg Square in Boston, no single one of the red brick houses . . . is so remarkable as to warrant preservation apart from its surroundings, yet the whole is considerably greater than the sum of its parts.

—Walter Muir Whitehill, "The Right of Cities to be Beautiful," *With Heritage So Rich*

DISTRICTS. A district is an area with a special character. That character sets it apart from its surroundings so that intuitively you know when you are in the midst of it.

District character comes from features recurring throughout the district. Typically it is some combination of similarities—similarities in building scale, materials, architectural styles, details; in landscaping, topography, streetscape; in how buildings

Overleaf and above: Twickenham Historic District, Huntsville. An exceptional concentration of antebellum houses, some dating from before Alabama statehood, sets Twickenham apart. Refined Federal style residences from Huntsville's earliest decades mix with later Greek Revival, Victorian, and Craftsman bungalow styles, unified by their similar scale and relation to the street. Several churches and a smattering of offices add variety. In keeping with the district character described in the National Register nomination as "a museum of architecture spanning sixteen decades," houses continue to be built, guided by a design review process established in 1972. Altogether there are some 350 structures in the tree-lined district, all within strolling distance of downtown's courthouse square. NR

relate to the street and to one another. The accumulation of these features—often over an extended period of time, rooted in a common development history—creates a distinctive look and feel. And yet within the overall consistency there may be great variety and diversity. Everything need not look exactly the same.

Smells and sounds may also contribute to district character. Think of a coastal district known for its fish markets, or a district where coffee roasters or bakeries are concentrated, or one adjacent to a railroad or industrial site filled with penetrating smells and clanging sounds.

Recognition of districts as community-enriching entities broke new ground in the 1930s when Charleston and New Orleans pioneered local designation and protection of historic districts. They pushed the scope of preservation beyond single buildings to include entire residential and commercial neighborhoods. In so doing, they gave new status to areas whose overall character and sense of place was greater than the significance of their individual buildings. Although an area need not be historic to constitute a district, distinctive character often derives from authenticity and cohesiveness accrued over many generations, what noted preservationist William Murtagh called the "interplay of time, tradition and continued mutual existence."

Districts expand the visual interest and pleasure of a place into everyday settings where people live and work. A district may have a landmark or center or path within its bounds, or it may unify the area that lies between them. A district may function as a community within a larger city, such as the Battery in Charleston, Beacon Hill in Boston, or Georgetown in Washington, D.C. Sometimes a district may encompass an entire community, such as the village of Mooresville in north Alabama.

If a community lacks DISTRICTS with a special character and sense of place, it lacks broad areas of appealing ambience and unity that enrich community life. What are the districts in your community?

Visual unity characterizes the buildings around the Limestone County Courthouse, *related by their similar height, proportions,*

materials, and architectural details. Despite a few glaringly remodeled facades and out-of-character doors and windows, the district

around the square reminds us of its early days. The massing of the imposing county courthouse and of the First Presbyterian Church

with its striking steeple (not pictured) contrasts with the prevailing cohesiveness of the rest of the structures.

Courthouse Square, Athens. *Limestone County Courthouse, 1916-19, Bem Price, architect.* NR

The buildings along Anniston's Noble Street represent every decade of the city's development history, starting in the 1880s. Planners designed the street to be the commercial spine of a model industrial city. Today, revitalization efforts are finding success, aided by tax credits for rehabilitating historic buildings, an active Main Street program, and the special appeal of some of the architecture.

Noble Street, Anniston. NR

Steeply pitched gables create a memorable impression as you drive through Brantley

on the way to Florida beaches. Repetition of the distinctive form unifies this stretch of

mostly Victorian cottages, with their variety of welcoming porches set close to the street.

It is easy to imagine local carpenters creating this comfortable cohesiveness, as the town

took shape around the turn of the twentieth century. And today these houses—largely

unspoiled by character-destroying improvements—retain the authenticity of their

beginnings.

Houses on Main Street, Brantley. Buster Wyatt, Bill Harrington, carpenters for some of the

cottages. NR

Although almost brand new, Mt Laurel is designed to be an old-fashioned small town. So far, Elton B. Stephens, Jr.'s development near a high-growth corridor south of Birmingham includes a town center, two schools, several parks, and a variety of house types. Its hallmarks are its great sensitivity to the topography and natural landscape and its use of traditional forms and materials for all the buildings. Sidewalks and porches throughout the development encourage walking and nurture a sense of community.

Town of Mt Laurel, Shelby County, 1998–. Duany Plater-Zyberk & Co., Miami, master planner; Rip Weaver, ASLA, landscape architect; J. Scott Finn, director of design; Town Builders, Inc., contractor. Other architects for buildings pictured here and on page 97 (top): Dungan & Nequette Architects; Henry Sprott Long & Associates, Architects, in association with ArchitectureWorks, LLP; Looney Ricks Kiss, Architects, Inc., Memphis.

Two churches create an atmosphere of timeless serenity. Related for more than a century by their steeples, their missions, and their proximity, the charming Methodist church and its Baptist counterpart remind us of the importance of religious life in a small Southern town. Today shared services on alternating Sundays help sustain the churches as well as the community, which is losing population to cities where there are jobs.

Methodist and Baptist Churches, Pittsview. Pittsview United Methodist Church, ca. 1893, William Marshall Burt, master carpenter. Pittsview Baptist Church, 1897.

A public park surrounded by Victorian houses defines a neighborhood's character and communal life. For generations, nearby residents have treated Washington Square as their outdoor living room, enjoying its central fountain and picturesque iron deer set amongst azaleas, palmettos, and aged oaks. The park is the heart of Mobile's Oakleigh Garden District, a rich assemblage of nineteenth and twentieth-century homes named after the oldest house in the district, Oakleigh, now a house museum a few blocks from the square.

Washington Square, Mobile. *Land donated to the city as a park in 1850. Deer, cast by Wood & Perot Iron Works, Philadelphia; placed in Bienville Square 1858; relocated to Washington Square 1890.* NR

EDGES & G

ATEWAYS

The District of Columbia's Georgetown . . . is very neatly defined by natural and man-made boundaries. The natural boundaries are a creek on the eastern edge of the neighborhood and the Potomac River on the southern edge. The two man-made boundaries are Georgetown University and Hospital on the west and Dumbarton Oaks Estate and Montrose Park on the north.

—WILLIAM J. MURTAGH, *Keeping Time: The History and Theory of Preservation in America*

EDGES & GATEWAYS. Edges mark the bounds of a community. Gateways mark its points of entry. They are the means of delineating a town or a city or a neighborhood—of defining it as a separate entity.

The use of walls and gates to set a community apart dates back to ancient times. Well into the Middle Ages, walls continued to be built for defense with gates to control access. At the same time, the walls established community domain and the gates sometimes symbolized the community itself or its ruling authority. Eventually, as cities grew beyond their walls, these edges and gateways lost their functional value and were absorbed into the fabric of the larger city as historical remnants.

Overleaf and above: Edmund Pettus Bridge, Selma, 1938-40. At the river's edge, the community begins. The Alabama River was antebellum Selma's primary link to markets for its thriving cotton trade and the world beyond. A bridge became a new gateway in the 1880s, later superseded by the larger, more modern Edmund Pettus Bridge. On March 7, 1965, the Pettus bridge took on a different meaning, when state troopers and sheriff's deputies attacked civil rights marchers headed to Montgomery to protest unfair voting practices. Two weeks after that "Bloody Sunday" attack, the historic march crossed the bridge again, this time reaching its destination and giving impetus to passage of the Voting Rights Act of 1965. H. K. Stephenson, Alabama Highway Dept. bridge designer; T. A. Loving Co., Goldsboro, North Carolina, contractor. NHT

Although one would be hard-pressed today to find cities actually defined by walls and gates, especially within the United States, some smaller residential developments and colleges still use them as devices to declare their communities' presence and bounds. In addition to walls, a body of water or another large natural feature, a highway, or a railroad track may also serve as a community-defining edge—a line that helps differentiate a particular settled area from the territory around it. Edges visible

from a distance often provide striking community images. Think of Chicago's Lake Michigan shoreline, or the view of Jackson Square from the Mississippi River at New Orleans, or the New York skyline seen from the southern tip of Manhattan. While some edges are primarily visual, others, such as a busy highway or a broad river, may establish real barriers to coming and going. Some edges function simultaneously as a border and as a path that links different districts.

Today community gateways are usually symbolic. They can help create strong impressions of a place, such as the colorful Chinatown gates in San Francisco, Boston, Philadelphia, and Washington, D.C. Some cities and neighborhoods mark primary entrances and edges with distinctive signage or banners.

One note of caution about a recent trend involving walls and gates: gated residential enclaves, when they are exclusive and tightly restrict access, can seem to turn their backs on the communities within which they sit, rather than being an integral part of them.

When a community has features that function as EDGES and GATEWAYS, they reinforce awareness of the community as a special place. Are there edges and gateways in your community?

Gates and walls delineate the edge *that long separated the University of Montevallo campus from the surrounding residential neighborhood. The materials blend with the historic buildings and streets of the old campus, and the scale mediates sensitively between institution and neighborhood. Although university functions now occupy some of the houses, the residential character remains, preserving a sense of place.*

University of Montevallo Gates, Montevallo. *Given by the classes of 1937, 1938, 1939, and 1967.*

Town and gown meet at Toomer's

Corner in Auburn, at the intersection

of Magnolia Avenue and College Street.

A symbolic brick gateway and the

drugstore on the opposite corner mark

the edges where university and town life

come together. The spot is known for the

fresh lemonade served at the drugstore's

old-fashioned soda fountain and for the

exuberant celebrations of Auburn football

victories known as "rolling Toomer's."

Toomer's Corner, Auburn. *Gate given by the class of 1917, eagles given by a member of the class of 1931.*

Buildings and train tracks mark the edge *of Opelika's historic commercial district.*

The railroad made the city a lively east Alabama trade center and sparked development

of the late nineteenth and early twentieth-century buildings facing the tracks. Now

rehabilitation of those buildings is part of an effort to bring renewed vitality to the

community.

South Railroad Avenue, Opelika. NR

Train depots have long been symbolic gateways to the communities they serve. Although rail passengers no longer stop here,

the Evergreen Depot continues to play a key role in community life as the office for the Evergreen/Conecuh Chamber of Commerce

and the Conecuh County Economic Development Authority. And freight trains continue to rumble by, linking the area to markets

and fueling its economy.

Louisville and Nashville Depot, Evergreen, 1907-1908. *Goodwyn, Mills & Cawood, Inc., renovation architect; Duncan Builders, renovation*

contractor, 1998. NR

Tile-roofed gate houses with fluted Doric columns *and a sign arching above urn-topped posts mark the main entrance to Ashland*

Place, Mobile's finest early twentieth-century suburb. The architect incorporated benches in the gate houses and along the curving

walls for waiting streetcar riders. Along the residential community's southern edge, three more modest vehicular and pedestrian

gateways provide entry.

Ashland Place Entrance Gates, Mobile, ca. 1907. *Attributed to George B. Rogers, architect. NR*

122

123

In the heart of a small-scale early-to-mid-twentieth-century neighborhood, between

a cluster of stores and surrounding houses, Dawson Memorial Baptist Church has built

a large campus. The Family Recreation Center defines its eastern edge. The architect

used glass to help reduce the building's mass and to open it visually to the community,

responding to neighborhood concerns about the impact of expansion and the differences

in institutional and residential scale.

Dawson Family Recreation Center, Homewood, 1998-99. *Giattina Aycock Architecture*

Studio, architect; Doster Construction Co., Inc., contractor.

Strong edges express community *at the Alabama School of Fine Arts. With an entire city block available, the architect massed the*

building along the elevated interstate on the north side, defining an edge of the city center as well as the school. On the east side,

the massing establishes the school's presence in the urban fabric. Gabled rooftops provide a distinctive cap, whether viewed from the

ground or from nearby skyscrapers. They also allude to the school's residential character, housing students in the midst of downtown.

On the southern edge a setback creates a block-long oasis of green in the city.

Alabama School of Fine Arts, Birmingham, 1991-93. *Renneker, Tichansky & Associates, Inc., architect; Brice Building Co., Inc., contractor. Subsequent additions, Renneker, Tichansky & Associates, Inc., architect; Brasfield & Gorrie, LLC, contractor, 1994-99.*

CONNECT

NG FABRIC

The "little" buildings of a neighborhood are of primary importance in its identification . . . Rows and blocks of less important buildings . . . create . . . continuity . . . Like the component parts of an orchestra, the lesser buildings and spaces create the symphonic sense of. . . neighborhood.

—WILLIAM J. MURTAGH, *Keeping Time: The History and Theory of Preservation in America*

CONNECTING FABRIC. Connecting fabric refers to buildings and landscapes that hold a community together visually. They are the underlying structure, the interlacing threads that make the cloth whole.

Connecting fabric is akin to districts, and in fact often contributes to district character. The difference between the two is a matter of focus. For a district, the focus is the area in its entirety. For connecting fabric, the focus is on the pieces that weave parts of the district together. The most familiar example of connecting fabric is a row of buildings standing side by side, joined by similarities in height, scale, and materials. We see the individual buildings, perhaps differing in style and architectural details, yet they all fit together. Water Avenue in Selma and Lower Commerce Street in Montgomery come readily to mind. Sometimes the connecting fabric is smaller-scale mid-block buildings that stretch between

Overleaf and above: North Prairie Street, Union Springs. Buildings related by scale and materials, by window patterns and decorative tops unify the commercial district that centers on the Bullock County Courthouse. They are a fitting setting to showcase the splendid Second Empire style courthouse in their midst. Behind the courthouse stands a brick jail with corner turrets that the community rallied to preserve as a museum when it was threatened with demolition for parking. Courthouse, 1871-72, M. M. Tye, architect and contractor; renovation and one-story wings, 1954, Carl Cooper, architect; Henderson, Bland and Green, contractor. Jail, 1897, Pauley Jail Building Co., Inc., St. Louis, Missouri, contractor. Bird Dog Field Trial Monument, Bob Wehle, sculptor. NR

prominent corner skyscrapers. In Savannah, the repetition

of the city's distinctive squares creates connection. In Paris,

where beige-toned facades help unify the entire city, color

plays a key role.

To maintain and renew a community's connecting

fabric requires that architects be willing to fit into an exist-

ing setting rather than impose a self-absorbed "signature"

building that prefers to stand alone. Architecture critic Paul

Goldberger had this in mind when he spoke of the impor-

tance of what he called "background buildings" and the need "to make decent, civilized, comfortable buildings that exist at

a high level of architectural seriousness but defer to a greater whole." He called these "the building blocks of a city."

Connecting fabric is lost when a building ignores its surroundings, or when a parking lot destroys a row of buildings.

This is why thoughtful urban designers seek to edge surface parking lots with a visual connection to nearby building fronts,

and to put street-level retail in parking decks to break up long stretches

of blank walls and encourage pedestrian activity.

Landscape is not always recognized as connecting fabric, but its

role is crucial. In a rural setting, where landscape is the dominant quality,

once that connecting fabric is destroyed, it is likely lost to us forever.

Scenic easements are a tool for protecting expanses of landscape. Sensi-

tive architects seek to let the character of the landscape endure by siting

buildings to fit into its natural contours and vegetation.

CONNECTING FABRIC helps hold a community together. Where

is the connecting fabric in your community?

131

A new neighborhood rises in downtown Birmingham. It takes its design cues from two historic schools nearby, incorporating their

red brick and gable and parapet forms into townhouses and flats. Stoops add a rhythmic accent to the architecture and strengthen

its urban residential character. Nearby amenities include a park, a YMCA youth development center, a community garden, and

the central public library, along with the two schools, one in operation and one awaiting a new use. When the final phase of the

HOPE VI project is complete, there will be more than six hundred housing units combining subsidized and market-rate rentals plus

some fifty townhouses for sale.

Park Place, Birmingham, 2004–. Williams Blackstock Architects, P.C., architect; Integral/Doster Metro Gardens Construction, a joint venture, contractor.

132

134

Sidewalks, trees, and porches knit a neighborhood together, *along with a variety of compatible architectural styles. In Decatur's historic Albany neighborhood, Colonial Revival and Queen Anne-influenced houses mix comfortably with Craftsman bungalows and other popular styles of the day. The planned community, a separate city until it became part of Decatur in 1927, was laid out by a landscape architect of national reputation. In recent decades the neighborhood has rallied to preserve its heritage and rehabilitate the large public park that has always been a focal point.*

Albany Historic District (New Decatur/Albany Residential Historic District), Decatur. *Town plan, 1887, Nathan Franklin Barrett, New York.* NR

An overarching canopy of live oaks becomes a visual metaphor for community coherence in Magnolia Springs. The quiet beauty

of the place, set on the Magnolia River in Baldwin County, has long attracted folks seeking a mild climate and relaxed way of life

in the midst of a bucolic landscape.

Oak Street Canopy, Magnolia Springs

137

Modest buildings march down

Guntersville's main street looking like

they belong together. They have stood

side by side for decades, their sheltering

awnings, brick facades, and similar

window patterns forming a pleasing

backdrop for the comings and goings of

daily life.

Gunter Avenue, Guntersville

A pair of church spires anchors one end of Cullman's downtown commercial district. One and two-story brick buildings line the streets, their facades enriched with cornices, corbeling, stringcourses, and other decorative treatments. Windows add rhythmic patterns except where they have been covered by incompatible remodeling. The train tracks that gave birth to the city in 1873, and were later lowered thirty feet so that trains would no longer interrupt traffic, run along the district's southwest edge.

Downtown Commercial District, Cullman. *Sacred Heart of Jesus Catholic Church, 1911-16; Old Federal Building, 1913-14.* NR

Wooden fences and tree-shaded lanes weave continuity into the fabric of a village that has changed little in size and layout since the 1840s. Generations of families are part of that fabric, along with their houses. The buildings enrich the pattern and texture of the place with the stories they hold and the ease with which they fit into their setting.

Town of Mooresville. NR

Family farms and small settlements typify Paint Rock Valley in the Appalachian foothills of northeast Alabama. The largely

pristine landscape is unmarred by major highways and sprawl development. As a result, the rural scenery still defines the valley and

connects us to its pioneer roots. Homesteads with barns and other outbuildings carry on the traditions and way of life established

by settlers after the Cherokee were forced to cede their land to the U.S. government in 1819. The threat of destructive development

has mobilized Jackson County Historical Association volunteers to document and try to preserve their special heritage.

Paint Rock Valley, Jackson County. *Ralph and Bessie Hall house, ca. 1900, John B. and Will Lanham, builders; Ike Erwin house, ca. 1900,
Ike Erwin, builder.*

MEANING

5 MAY 1963 BIRMINGHAM POLICE ATTACK MARCHING CHILDREN WITH DOGS AND FIREHOSES

WILLIAM LEWIS MOORE SLAIN DURING ... MARCH AGAINST SEGREGATION

11 JUN 1963 ALABAMA GOVERNOR STANDS IN SCHOOLHOUSE DOOR TO STOP UNIVERSITY INTEGRATION

12 JUN 1963 MEDGAR EVERS CIVIL RIGHTS LEADER ASSASSINATED JACKSON, MS

28 AUG 1963 250 000 AMERICANS MARCH ON WASHINGTON FOR CIVIL RIGHTS

15 SEP 1963 ADDIE MAE COLLINS, DENISE MCNAIR, CAROLE ROBERTSON, CYNTHIA WESLEY SCHOOLGIRLS KILLED IN BOMBING OF 16TH ST BAPTIST CHURCH, BIRMINGHAM, AL

15 SEP 1963 VIRGIL LAMAR WARE YOUTH KILLED DURING WAVE OF RACIST VIOLENCE BIRMINGHAM

23 JAN 1964 POLL TAX OUTLAWED IN FEDERAL ELEC...

31 JAN 1964 LOUIS ALLEN WITNESS TO MURDER OF... RIGHTS WORKER ASSASSINATED...

7 APR 1964 REV BRUCE KLUNDE... CONSTRUCTION OF SEG... CLEVELAND OH

2 MAY 1964 HENRY ... MOORE KI...

20 ...

Man's most fundamental need is to experience his existence as meaningful.

—Christian Norberg-Schulz, *Genius Loci: Towards a Phenomenology of Architecture*

MEANING. When a place represents a significant event or experience or person, it has meaning.

The meaning may be personal, such as an experience of grief or joy or inspiration. Think of a cemetery where loss came to rest, the church where marriage took place, a ball field or a summer camp where friendships blossomed or a childhood lesson was learned. The meaning may also be collective, a cultural memory shared by an entire community, or even a state or a nation. Birmingham's Sixteenth Street Baptist Church, where four young girls lost their lives during the civil rights movement, and New York City's Ground Zero, where the World

Overleaf and right: Civil Rights Memorial, Montgomery, 1988-89. Water washes slowly over the names of those who died during the struggle for civil rights. The facts of their death are cut into the granite along with a chronology of the movement's milestone events. The elemental use of water, with its barely perceptible motion and symbolic cleansing, heightens the emotional engagement of those who come here to honor the dead. At the dedication, tears of victims' families blended with the water to become part of the memorial.

Maya Lin, designer; W. K. Upchurch Construction Co., Inc., contractor.

Trade Center towers once stood, are places that hold powerful collective meaning.

Places that embody meaning can link us to the past and to the future. They rekindle the memory of times and people who have gone before us and bring that memory into the present. By caring for the place and keeping alive the memories that it holds, we connect to the underlying experience of humanity. And we enable those who follow us to make the same connection.

Some designers of public spaces, alert to the power of meaning, seek to incorporate references to a community's roots in their work, to keep its stories alive. They find a variety of ways to enrich the public realm. In the process they add interest, insight, and sometimes humor to a community's street life. One such example is Asheville, North Carolina's Urban Trail, a walking trail that functions as a history and art museum without walls. A variety of other examples appear in the book *Place Makers: Public Art That Tells You Where You Are* by Ronald Lee Fleming and Renata von Tscharner.

MEANING adds depth to the way we experience our communities. What places give your community meaning?

Recalling a young life lost and a company town now gone, the Howard Gardner Nichols Memorial Library remains, today serving genealogists rather than mill workers. It is named for the young Massachusetts industrialist who came south to supervise construction of the Dwight Textile Mill and plan a model village for its workers. He was killed in an accident not long after the mill went into operation. His mother and his father, an officer of Dwight Manufacturing Company, gave the library in his memory.

Northeast Alabama Howard Gardner Nichols Memorial Historical and Genealogical Library (Howard Gardner Nichols Memorial Library, Alabama City Library), Gadsden, ca. 1901-1902. *Possibly by a Boston architect; construction said to be by mill employees.* NR

THIS BUILDING WAS ERECTED
BY THE DWIGHT MANUFACTURING
COMPANY AS A MEMORIAL
TO
HOWARD GARDNER NICHOLS
UNDER WHOSE SUPERVISION
THIS TOWN WAS LAID OUT,
AND FIRST MILL CONSTRUCTED.
BORN AT HAVERHILL, MASS.,
APRIL 16 1871.
GRADUATED FROM HARVARD UNIVERSITY
1893
DIED JUNE 23, 1896
FROM THE EFFECT OF INJURIES RECEIVED
WHILE IN THE DISCHARGE OF HIS DUTIES.
BELOVED AND LAMENTED HIS MEMORY
LIVES TO BLESS THIS COMMUNITY.

Marking long-held values, *the Wilcox Female Institute signifies a community's*

dedication to education and local heritage. It was chartered in 1850 to educate daughters

of planters and other well-to-do citizens and then in 1908 it became a public school.

The threat of demolition in the 1970s rallied citizens to form the Wilcox Historical

Society, which now owns and preserves the building.

Wilcox Female Institute, Camden, 1849. *Luther Hill & Associates, architect; Chapman Design*
& Construction Co., contractor, phase I restoration, 1970s. NR, HABS

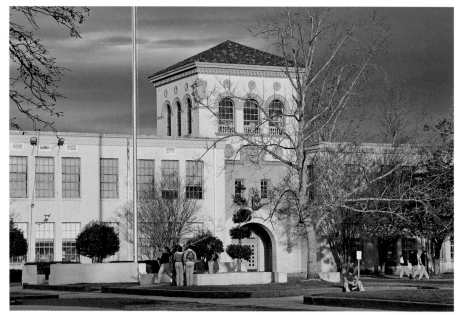

RICH with history and tradition, Murphy High School is an exceptional place. *The campus of distinguished Spanish Revival*

style buildings not only defines an educational community but also exhibits a level of quality that carries over into academics and

energizes school spirit and alumni involvement. While numerous families have multigenerational ties to the school, the place has

changed with the times and serves an economically and ethnically diverse student body. At a point when educators are rethinking

the benefits of abandoning neighborhood schools for large consolidated schools, Murphy—with some 2,500 students—proves a

contrary model with a proud legacy.

Murphy High School, Mobile, 1925-26, 1930. *Perkins, Fellows & Hamilton, Chicago, architect; George B. Rogers, architect, construction supervisor;*
B. E. Buffaloe and Co., Memphis, contractor. Alterations and additions by various other architects and contractors through the years. NR

156

Though its congregation is long gone, Pleasant Hill Presbyterian Church is still part of the community that once thrived in this remote rural setting. Graves in the adjoining cemetery, beginning in the 1830s, tell of the lives of nearby settlers. Some of their descendants continue to care for the place. Efforts have also been made to preserve the church, whose domed belfry and recessed portico reflect the elevated tastes a booming cotton economy brought to the hinterland not long before the Civil War.

Pleasant Hill (Mount Carmel) Presbyterian Church & Cemetery, Dallas and Lowndes Counties, 1852. NR

A breathtaking expanse of art glass brings inspiration to Jasper's First United Methodist Church. The celestial images of angels and cherubs, traditional messengers of God, add meaning to the great domed space, as does the shared worship of many decades. Meaning also comes from historical associations: five U.S. Congressmen have been active members of the church, including Speaker of the U.S. House of Representatives William B. Bankhead, who was buried from the church in 1940, with President Franklin D. Roosevelt, members of his cabinet, and Sen. Harry S. Truman among the dignitaries in attendance.

First United Methodist Church, Jasper, 1916-21. *J. A. Smith, contractor; A. Leyendecker, St. Joseph Art Glass Co., St. Joseph, Missouri, dome design.* NR, HABS

A community persists through time in Selma's Old Live Oak Cemetery. The gravestones provide glimpses of lives that once gave vitality to this part of the Black Belt, including a U.S. vice president, U.S. senators, Confederate generals, and Alabama's first black congressman, along with countless others remembered and forgotten. This is also a gathering place for the living. They come here to visit loved ones, to search for nuggets of history, and to absorb the tranquility of the enduring oaks and magnolias.

Old Live Oak Cemetery, Selma. NR

The camp house reveals the essence of Dollarhide—*in a screened porch where a casual cluster of chairs awaits conversation, in photograph-lined walls where one can spot the faces of grandfathers and great-grandfathers in hunting parties of the 1920s, in a well-stocked trophy room where members indulge their trademark sociability, with vigorous kidding back and forth, sitting around the fireplace and card table. Tradition and camaraderie are at the core of the hunting club whose roots go back to 1889. The forty members pride themselves on keeping the customs alive, including a strong commitment to conservation and, in season, deer drives with dogs and shotguns. Club members hunt and fish on roughly 6,000 acres associated with the camp.*

Dollarhide Camp, Greene County. *Camp house, 1926.*

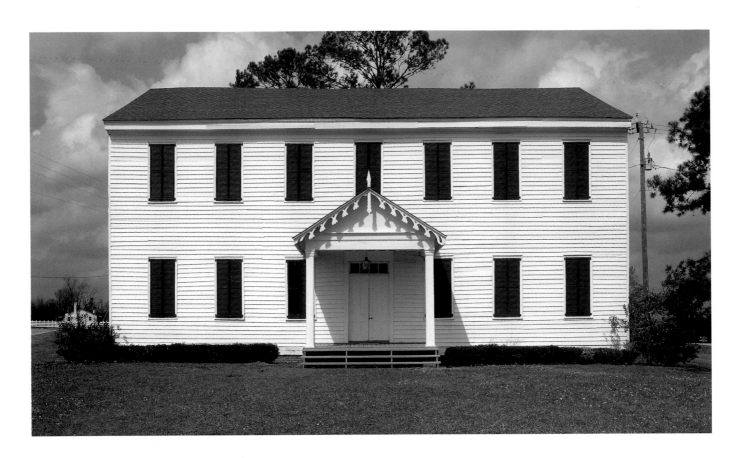

The oldest building in Monroe County tells of community life in a new state. Constructed around 1824 for Masonic Lodge No. 3, the building served as a church, a courtroom, and a place of general assembly, in addition to housing the fraternal organization's meetings on the upper floor. The Marquis de Lafayette, who like George Washington and Benjamin Franklin was a Freemason, visited here in 1825 during his celebrated thirteen-month tour of the United States. The upstairs room still speaks of its Masonic past, though the structure is now seriously threatened by deterioration. The building was moved from its original site in Claiborne in 1884.

Masonic Lodge, Perdue Hill, ca. 1824. *John Parks, superintendent of construction. Portico, late 1800s, presumably added after 1884 move from Claiborne.*
Holmes & Holmes, Architects, restoration planning, 2006. HABS

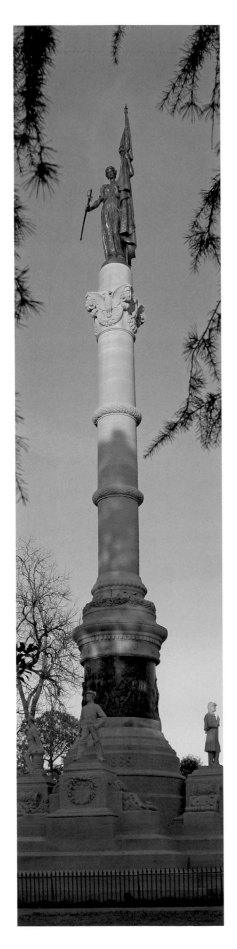

A work of art recalls a bloody war.

Bronze and granite sculptures add beauty to a colossal column commemorating the service and sacrifice of 122,000 Alabamians who fought in the Civil War. It stands next to the state Capitol, where Jefferson Davis took office as president of the Confederacy in 1861. Twenty-five years later he returned to lay the cornerstone of this monument, consecrated to the memory of Alabama soldiers and seamen.

Confederate Monument, Capitol Grounds, Montgomery, 1886-98.
Alexander Doyle, New York, designer/sculptor; Fred Barnicoat, Quincy, Massachusetts, granite statuary sculptor; Henry-Bonnard Bronze Co., New York, bronze casting; Curbow-Clapp Marble Co., Sinclair and Lawler, installation. McKay Lodge Fine Arts Conservation Laboratory, Inc., Oberlin, Ohio, conservation consultant; Conser-vation Solutions, Inc., Washington, D.C., conser-vation treatment, 2003. NR

CELEBRATING
COMMUNITY

We must ensure that what we build . . .will be worth remembering.

—RONALD LEE FLEMING AND RENATA VON TSCHARNER,

Place Makers: Public Art That Tells You Where You Are

WE HUMAN BEINGS first experienced community out of our need for one another. Individuals banded together for the most fundamental reason: to survive. The places they created expressed their mutual dependency and shared existence. In today's modern world, however, we are no longer so interdependent. Prosperity and our desire for self-expression have brought us many choices, which in turn can make it more difficult to create and sustain the kinds of communities that once came about naturally. But when we are motivated and succeed, we all benefit.

To create healthy communities takes enlightened planning along with involved citizens willing to work for the common good. With this foundation, architecture and land design can contribute to our ability to live together. Without it,

Overleaf and right: The Harbert Center, Birmingham, 1984-86. Designed to fit into the urban streetscape and provide versatile spaces for a variety of business, civic, and social gatherings, Birmingham's Harbert Center adds vitality to downtown life. John Harbert and Hall Thompson conceived the facility to be the headquarters of the downtown Birmingham Rotary, Kiwanis, and Crippled Children's Foundation/Quarterback clubs, as well as a prime meeting spot for other groups, and they led the fundraising to make it a reality.

Moss & Associates Architects, Inc./Renneker, Tichansky & Associates, Inc., a joint venture, architect; Harbert Construction Corp., contractor.

170

careless development decisions can fragment and destroy both the beauty and the function of our towns and cities and rural landscapes.

We have seen the results. The preceding chapters pay tribute to examples of design around the state that help define and contribute to the quality of community life in Alabama. In this chapter we celebrate more of these special places. We celebrate how design that meets community needs in large and small ways knits us together. We celebrate the values that these communities stand for. We celebrate the variety of ways we nurture community:

A library where young and old come for information and pleasure.

A meeting place for civic clubs that is a hub of downtown community.

An outdoor market that brings farmers and urban dwellers

together and helps sustain and enrich both ways of life.

A theater and concert hall where people come from near and far to

enjoy music, dance, drama, and entertainment.

A rural school that gave its community a proud tradition that lives on.

A children's zoo that appeals to families with a combination of education, exploration, and fun.

An old movie theater that local citizens are bringing back to life to serve new community needs.

A church with a rich heritage that shapes its identity in a small town.

A landscaped park that is an oasis of culture and beauty.

An old schoolhouse where home cooking nourishes community ties.

A new town center and an old town main street that are full of people and vitality.

What are the similar places where you live—places that celebrate community connectedness, past, present, and future—places that you can help support . . . or even help create?

Designed to showcase the performing arts and draw people from throughout the metropolitan area, the Alys Stephens Center succeeds with great flair. It combines superior performing venues, stylish spaces, and varied programming—from classical music to jazz, pop, and gospel, from dance to drama to big-name entertainers, plus popular arts education for all ages. Two theaters, a concert hall, and a recital hall share a grand lobby where audiences mingle. The center enlivens the cultural life of the region as well as the University of Alabama at Birmingham, where it is located.

Alys Robinson Stephens Performing Arts Center, Birmingham. *Phase I: Davis Architects, Inc., architect; Dunn Construction Co., Inc., building shell contractor, 1992-93; Taylor & Miree Construction, Inc., fit-up contractor, 1995-96. Phase II: KPS Group, Inc., architect; Duncan & Thompson Construction Services LLC, contractor, 1998-99. Phase III: KPS Group, architect; Richardson Construction Co., Inc., civil and structural contractor; Golden & Associates Construction, LLC, shell and fit-up contractor, 2003-2004. Sculpture by Frank Fleming.*

Landscape sculpts experience at Blount Cultural Park in Montgomery. *Though the park has expanded significantly since it was created for the Alabama Shakespeare Festival, the design concept of the original approach remains. A tree-lined road creates a transition to leave nearby suburban sprawl behind and prepare one for the cultural experiences that lie ahead. Rolling land and plantings hide the destination until a curve suddenly reveals it—a striking brick theater dramatically sited overlooking a lake. The site design uses roads and lakes as organizing devices and the landscape itself to unify the park's different precincts—theater and gardens, museum of fine arts. The result is a cultural setting with appeal to many ages and interests.*

Blount Cultural Park, Montgomery. *Master plan, Thomas Blount, 1982-2002; Russell Page, London, conceptual consultation, 1983-85. Landscape architecture, Reynolds & Jewell Landscape Architecture, Raleigh, 1982-87; Edwina von Gal + Co., New York, 1994-2001. Carolyn Blount Theatre, 1982-85, Thomas Blount, AIA, and L. Perry Pittman, architects; Blount International, LTD, contractor. Sculpture of Wynton M. Blount by Charles Parks, Wilmington, Delaware.*

A new development redefines Homewood's city center. Public and private sectors partnered to build a city hall and civic plaza flanked by restaurants, shops, and residential condominiums, all supported by six hundred parking spaces on and below grade. Differentiated massing and materials help relate the complex to the scale of the surrounding commercial area, while the mix of uses generates activity that enlivens the streetscape and spills over to adjacent businesses.

Soho Square, Homewood, 2004-2006. Cohen Carnaggio Reynolds, architect; McCrory Building Co., Inc., contractor, Homewood City Hall, 2004-2005; Brasfield & Gorrie, LLC, contractor, parking deck, plaza, Soho Flats, retail shell, 2004-2006.

The cool shade of the monumental arbor at the Birmingham Children's Zoo *is a favorite gathering spot for families. Parents relax while watching children play in the water fountains, climb the mountain, explore fossils, and discover the underwater life of a local stream. Through five acres of interactive exhibits and engaging public space, the Children's Zoo builds community interest in and knowledge of Alabama's extraordinary biodiversity and the importance of conserving it.*

Junior League of Birmingham–Hugh Kaul Children's Zoo, Birmingham. *Giattina Aycock Architecture Studio, master planner and architect; Ross Land Design, P.C., landscape architect; Golden & Associates Construction, LLC, phase I contractor, 2001-2002; Hoar Construction, LLC, phase II construction manager, 2004-2005.*

Saturdays from May to October, thousands of Birmingham-area residents converge at Pepper Place to shop for local produce, flowers, baked goods, and honey. Adding to the ambience are the sounds of area musicians and tantalizing aromas from cooking demonstrations given by leading city chefs. The backdrop is a former Dr. Pepper syrup plant whose bold sign inspired the name of the design-oriented retail and office complex that surrounds the market.

Pepper Place Saturday Market, Birmingham, 1990. *Dr. Pepper Syrup Plant, 1931, D. O. Whilldin, architect; Southern Construction Co., contractor.* NR

With the help of a harmonious rear addition, *Eufaula's Carnegie Library is in its second century of community service. The library epitomizes the philanthropic vision of industrialist Andrew Carnegie, who helped fund the construction of some 2,500 public libraries in the United States and other English-speaking countries. Besides offering free access to books, the library provided a center for many cultural, social, and political events in its second-floor auditorium. Of the fourteen Carnegie libraries built in Alabama, only those in Eufaula and Union Springs continue to function as libraries.*

Eufaula Carnegie Library, Eufaula, 1904. *Charles A. Stephens, architect; Algernon Blair, contractor. Blondheim & Mixon, Inc., architect; Russell Construction, contractor, 1989-90 addition.* NR

Prominently sited at a bend in Broad Street, *the Art Deco style Pitman Theatre*

brought a touch of modernity to downtown Gadsden in the late 1940s. The neon-lit sign

and marquee heightened its visibility as a destination for enjoying the latest films in

air-conditioned comfort. Today the community is finding new uses to keep the building

an active part of life on the city's main street. A courtyard has added an inviting outdoor

space between the theater and the adjacent Senior Activity Center, the lobby is being

renovated as a welcome center and transportation museum for Etowah County, and

the auditorium will eventually be used for concerts, lectures, and movies.

Pitman Theatre, Gadsden, 1946-47. *D. O. Whilldin, architect.* NR

A Rosenwald school in Bullock County *stands for a remarkable program to educate African-Americans in the segregated South. Booker T. Washington originated the model when he started building rural schools using standardized plans, with the requirement that the community cover a significant share of the cost. However, it was Chicago philanthropist Julius Rosenwald, president of Sears, Roebuck and Company, who brought Washington's efforts to fruition on a grand scale, eventually giving seed money for almost five thousand schools in fifteen states. The Merritt School is one of only about fifteen Alabama schools found remaining of almost four hundred built between 1913 and 1932. Enlarged twice, it continues to serve its community with programs for nutrition, literacy, health education, and adult education and as a site for community meetings.*

Old Merritt School, Midway, ca. 1922. *From plans by Samuel L. Smith. Additions ca. 1935; ca. 1946. NR*

At Morning Star Baptist Church in Demopolis, *arches shape the interior space. They embrace the congregation and help direct the focus of worship to the pulpit, cross, and altar. The building is from a design by Wallace A. Rayfield, a talented black architect best known for his Sixteenth Street Baptist Church in Birmingham. Morning Star traces its roots to the first Missionary Baptist Church in Marengo County.*

Morning Star Baptist Church, Demopolis, 1914-20. *Wallace A. Rayfield, architect; Reverend General Harrison Black, contractor/builder.*

Off the beaten path, a schoolhouse turned restaurant is still a hub of community in south Montgomery County. It was first a center of learning for young African Americans, beginning around 1910. Well-worn blackboards and portraits of the U. S. Presidents remain from those times, but since 1985 visitors have flocked here not to study but to feast on down-home cooking and Southern hospitality. Besides fresh vegetables grown by the owner, the restaurant's specialties include an apple cheese casserole and fried okra that are among the Alabama Bureau of Tourism & Travel's "100 dishes to eat in Alabama before you die."

Red's Little Schoolhouse (Hills Chapel Community School), south Montgomery County, ca. 1910

Historic buildings filled with locally owned businesses *give authenticity to Northport's small-town charm. Boosted by the popular Kentuck Festival of the Arts that attracts thousands of visitors every fall and has prompted a year-round market for local art galleries, Northport's economy benefits from the town's appealing ambience and proximity to Tuscaloosa. A downtown plan with street improvements in the 1990s reinforced the character and community spirit of the place.*

Main Avenue, Northport. *Downtown plan and streetscape improvements, Philip B. Prigmore & Albert L. Fortner: Preservation, Planning, and Design, Alfred, New York, planner/designer; John Plott Co., Inc., contractor, phase I, 1996, phase II, 1999. NR*

MAP OF THE SITES

AUTAUGA COUNTY
Prattville (1)
West Main Street

BALDWIN COUNTY
Malbis (2)
Malbis Memorial Church
Magnolia Springs (3)
Oak Street Canopy
Point Clear (4)
Public Walkway

BARBOUR COUNTY
Eufaula (5)
East Broad Street
Eufaula Carnegie Library

BLOUNT COUNTY
Horton Mill Covered Bridge
(6)

BULLOCK COUNTY
Midway (7)
Old Merritt School
Union Springs (8)
North Prairie Street
Wayman Chapel A.M.E.
Church

BUTLER COUNTY
Greenville (9)
Butler County Courthouse

CALHOUN COUNTY
Chief Ladiga Trail (10)
Anniston (11)
Noble Street

CLAY COUNTY
Ashland (12)
Clay County Courthouse

CLEBURNE COUNTY
Chief Ladiga Trail (13)

CONECUH COUNTY
Evergreen (14)
Louisville and Nashville
Depot

COOSA COUNTY
Goodwater (15)
Goodwater Feed & Hardware

CRENSHAW COUNTY
Brantley (16)
Houses on Main Street

CULLMAN COUNTY
Cullman (17)
Downtown Commercial
District

DALLAS COUNTY
Pleasant Hill Presbyterian
Church & Cemetery (18)
Selma (19)
Edmund Pettus Bridge
Old Live Oak Cemetery
St. James Hotel

ELMORE COUNTY
Wetumpka (20)
Bibb Graves Bridge

ETOWAH COUNTY
Gadsden (21)
Howard Gardner Nichols
Memorial Historical and
Genealogical Library
Pitman Theatre

GREENE COUNTY
Dollarhide Camp (22)
Eutaw (23)
Courthouse Square

HALE COUNTY
Newbern (24)
Town Center

JACKSON COUNTY
Paint Rock Valley (25)
Russell Cave National
Monument (26)

JEFFERSON COUNTY
Birmingham (27)
Alabama School of Fine Arts
Alys Robinson Stephens Per-
forming Arts Center
The Harbert Center
Junior League of Birmingham-
Hugh Kaul Children's Zoo
Most Worshipful Prince Hall
Grand Lodge
Park Place
Pepper Place Saturday Market
Rickwood Field
SawWorks Studio
UAB Campus Recreation
Center
Vulcan Statue and Park
Homewood (28)
Dawson Family Recreation
Center

Homewood Shades Creek
Greenway
Soho Square
Mountain Brook (29)
Mountain Brook Walkways

LAUDERDALE COUNTY
Florence (30)
Trowbridge's

LEE COUNTY
Auburn (31)
Toomer's Corner
Opelika (32)
South Railroad Avenue

LIMESTONE COUNTY
Athens (33)
Founders Hall, Athens State
University
Courthouse Square
Mooresville (34)
Town of Mooresville

LOWNDES COUNTY
Hayneville (35)
Lowndes County Courthouse

MACON COUNTY
Little Texas Methodist Taber-
nacle and Campground (36)
Tuskegee (37)
Tuskegee University Historic
Campus

MADISON COUNTY
Huntsville (38)
Big Spring International Park
Marshall Space Flight Center
Main Administrative Com-
plex
Twickenham Historic District

MARENGO COUNTY
Demopolis (39)
Morning Star Baptist Church
Public Square

MARSHALL COUNTY
Guntersville (40)
Gunter Avenue
U.S. Post Office

MOBILE COUNTY
Mobile (41)
Ashland Place Entrance Gates
GM&O Building
Murphy High School

National African-American
Archives & Museum
Spring Hill College
Quadrangle
Washington Square
Wayfinding System

MONTGOMERY COUNTY
Red's Little School House (42)
Montgomery (43)
Blount Cultural Park
Civil Rights Memorial
Confederate Monument
Garrett Coliseum
Houghton Memorial Library,
Huntingdon College
Montgomery Curb Market

MONROE COUNTY
Monroeville (44)
Old Monroe County Court-
house
Perdue Hill (45)
Masonic Lodge

MORGAN COUNTY
Decatur (46)
Albany Historic District
Princess Theatre

RUSSELL COUNTY
Pittsview (47)
Methodist and Baptist
Churches

SHELBY COUNTY
Montevallo (48)
University of Montevallo
Gates
Mt Laurel (49)
Town of Mt Laurel

TUSCALOOSA COUNTY
Northport (50)
Main Avenue

WALKER COUNTY
Jasper (51)
First United Methodist
Church

WILCOX COUNTY
Camden (52)
Wilcox Female Institute

WINSTON COUNTY
Double Springs (53)
Winston County Courthouse

194

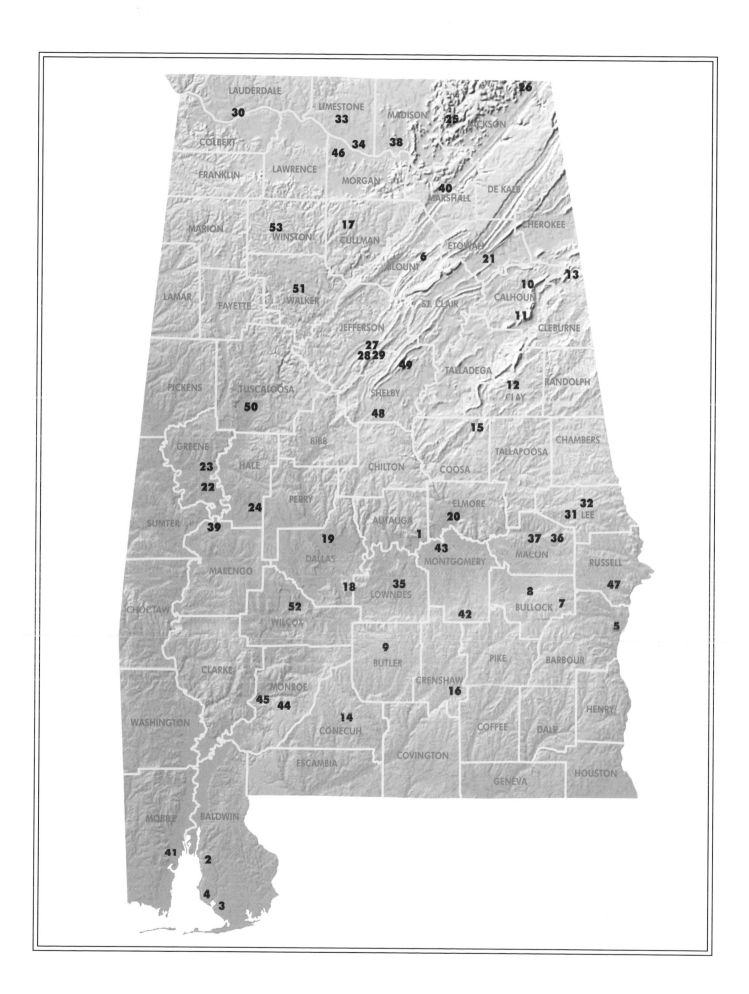

G L O S S A R Y

arcade   A series of arches on *piers* or columns

axis   An imaginary line about which parts of a building or the main elements of a site are disposed, usually with careful attention to symmetry

beam   A horizontal, weight-supporting member of a structural frame

Beaux Arts style   A classical style of the late nineteenth and early twentieth centuries that takes its name from the École des Beaux Arts in Paris; it is characterized by grandiose compositions, often featuring monumental, frequently paired columns, central *pavilions*, raised basements, and exuberant classical detail

belfry   A bell tower, especially one surmounting another structure

brace   A straight or arched diagonal support designed to strengthen the framing system of a roof

Byzantine   Architecture associated with the Byzantine empire after Constantine moved the capital of the Roman empire to Byzantium, often related to the Eastern Orthodox Church and its traditions; characterized by massive domes with square bases and round arches, rich ornamentation, and mosaics

classical, classicism   Relating to the principles of design and proportion as well as the forms and details found in ancient Greek and Roman architecture

cloister   A quadrangle or open courtyard enclosed by a covered passage, one side of which is usually an open *arcade* or *colonnade*; seen in medieval monasteries

Colonial Revival style   A loosely defined style that used forms and details inspired by early American architecture of the eighteenth and the first part of the nineteenth century

colonnade   A row of columns carrying an *entablature* or arches

corbeling   A bracket form usually produced by extending successive courses of masonry upward and outward from the wall surface

cornice   The projecting ornamental molding used to crown a building or to define the meeting of wall and ceiling; in classical architecture, the uppermost projecting section of an *entablature*, often decorated with moldings and *dentils* on its lower face

Craftsman bungalow   Typically a one-story house with a broad, gently pitched roof and rich use of materials and textures such as fieldstone, cobblestone, brick, clapboard, and shingles; one of the most frequently seen examples has paired front-facing *gables*, with the smaller, lower gable covering the porch and the larger gable spreading across the width of the house

cupola   A small, usually domed structure surmounting a roof

dentils   A series of small rectangular blocks frequently incorporated in the lower part of a classical *cornice*

Doric   See *order*

dormer   A window that projects through the slope of a roof

entablature   In classical architecture, the horizontal elements of an *order* that rest on the columns; it consists of the architrave (the lowest part of the entablature), the frieze (the middle part), and the *cornice* (the crowning part)

Federal style   A restrained, refined style popular in the United States from the late eighteenth century into the early nineteenth century; characterized by delicate lines and scale, smooth walls largely unadorned except for the entrance, low *hipped roofs*, and frequent use of semicircular and elliptical forms

gable   The triangular segment of a wall that supports the ends of a pitched roof

Gothic, Gothic Revival style   Relating to the architectural style prevalent in western Europe during the Middle Ages until the advent of the Renaissance, or to subsequent revival styles derived from medieval Gothic; pointed arches and stone tracery were characteristic features

Greek Revival style   A neoclassical style influenced by classical Greek architecture and popular in the United States in the mid-nineteenth century; characterized by symmetry, columns and *pilasters*, rectilinear lines, and a generally heavy scale expressed in *entablatures* and moldings

196

hammerbeam truss A framework of timbers for supporting a roof that takes its name from the hammerbeam, a short beam projecting from an interior wall, which is supported from below by a hammer *brace* and itself supports an arched timber or a post above

hipped roof A roof with four uniformly pitched sides

Ionic See *order*

mansard roof A roof with a steep, nearly vertical slope topped by a much-shallower pitched or nearly flat slope; named after French architect François Mansart

massing The shape of a building considered in three-dimensional volume as opposed to silhouette or decorative elements

mullion A slender vertical member that divides sections of a multipart window or door

order Any of several types of Greek or Roman classical columns, including their bases and *entablatures*. The primary orders are the Doric, Ionic, Corinthian, and Composite, with Greek and Roman variations, plus the Tuscan. The Greek **Doric** order is the heaviest and most massive; it is characterized by heavy fluted columns with no base, plain saucer-shaped capitals (the decorative top of a column), and a bold simple *cornice*. The **Ionic** order is characterized by its scroll-like capitals, called volutes. The **Corinthian** order is the most attenuated and richly embellished; it has a fluted column and a tall capital embellished with acanthus leaves ending in tight volutes in the four corners.

parapet A low wall at the edge of a roof, porch, or terrace

pavilion Usually referring to projecting central and/or end blocks of a building

pediment A wide, low-pitched *gable* surmounting the facade of a building in a classical style or above a portico, with the *cornice* molding enclosing the three sides of the triangle; any similar triangular crowning element used over doors, windows, and niches

pier A principal support, usually rectangular or square

pegged A method of joining wood using a wooden pin to fasten two members together

pilaster A shallow rectangular column or *pier* attached to a wall; often decorated to resemble a classical column

podium A raised base or platform that gives a structure greater visual monumentality

portico A porch with a roof supported by columns; usually the roof is *pedimented* and the columns are classical

post A vertical member of a structural frame

profile An outline, particularly the outline of the exposed face of a cross section

proportions Harmonious relations of parts to each other or to the whole

Queen Anne style A visually rich, exuberant style popular in the United States in the late nineteenth century; characterized by asymmetrical composition, irregular rooflines with towers and *turrets*, tall ornamental chimneys, varied surface textures and materials and colors, and wrap-around porches

ribbon windows A series of windows separated only by *mullions* to form a horizontal band

scale Relative size, such as the relationship of a building to those who view it, or to its surroundings or context

Spanish Revival style Architecture inspired by ornate Spanish colonial cathedrals such as that in Mexico City and by simpler frontier missions of the Southwest United States, among other sources; characterized by stucco or plaster walls, red-tile roofs, curvilinear roof *parapets*, and arched openings; popular in the early twentieth century

spire A roof structure tapering upward to a point

steeple The tower and *spire* of a church taken together

streetscape The appearance or view of a street encompassing the area between the buildings on opposite sides, including the building facades, sidewalks, signs, street furniture, landscaping, and other elements

stringcourse A horizontal band, usually masonry, on the exterior wall of a building

Town lattice truss A type of covered-bridge truss consisting of a lattice-like system of diagonals forming overlapping triangles, with no verticals; named for Ithiel Town who patented a lattice-truss design in 1820; it was popular because of the spans of which it was capable and the ease with which it could be erected in comparison to earlier methods

tracery Ornamental design of interlaced lines in the upper part of a *Gothic* window

turret A small, slender tower, sometimes *corbeled* out from the corner of a building

wayfinding A system of signage that navigates users through its "universe"—a city, a campus, an airport, a building, an exhibition; it facilitates arrival at the destination and helps users experience the environment in a positive way

SOURCES/BIBLIOGRAPHY

Sources Cited

Sources of quotations and references cited in each chapter essay appear below. References for the captions are in the Bibliography that follows.

FOREWORD—Lynch, Kevin. *The Image of the City.* Cambridge, Mass.: MIT Press, 1960, p. 1.

Whyte, William H. *City: Rediscovering the Center.* New York: Anchor Books / Doubleday, 1988.

CREATING COMMUNITY—Goldberger, Paul. *Buildings Against Cities: The Struggle to Make Places.* Birmingham, Ala.: Birmingham Historical Society and Harbert Corporation, 1989, p. 4.

Donne, John. "Meditation XVII." *Devotions Upon Emergent Occasions.*

LANDMARKS—Frazier, Ian. "Out of Ohio." *The New Yorker* 80, no. 42 (January 10, 2005), p. 40.

Muschamp, Herbert. "The Secret History of 2 Columbus Circle." *The New York Times* (Jan. 8, 2006).

IDENTITY—Naslund, Sena Jeter. *Four Spirits.* New York: Perennial / HarperCollins, 2003, p. 231.

CENTERS—Bunnell, Gene. *Making Places Special: Stories of Real Places Made Better by Planning.* Chicago: Planners Press, 2003, p. 84.

Goldberger, Paul. *Buildings Against Cities*, p. 12.

PATHS—Whyte, William H. *City: Rediscovering the Center.* New York: Anchor Books / Doubleday, 1988, p. 7.

Goldberger, Paul. *Buildings Against Cities*, p. 12.

Barnett, Jonathan. *Redesigning Cities: Principles, Pra tice, Implementation.* Chicago: Planners Press, 2003, p. 46.

DISTRICTS—Whitehill, Walter Muir. "The Right of Cities to be Beautiful." Special Committee on Historic Preservation, United States Conference of Mayors. Albert Rains and Laurance G. Henderson, eds. *With Heritage So Rich.* New York: Random House, 1966, p. 45.

Murtagh, William J. "Aesthetic and Social Dimensions of Historic Districts." In *Historic Districts: Identification, Social Aspects and Preservation,* 9-16. Washington, DC: National Trust for Historic Preservation, 1975, p. 11.

EDGES & GATEWAYS—Murtagh, William J. *Keeping Time: The History and Theory of Preservation in America.* 3rd ed. Hoboken, N. J.: John Wiley, 2006, p. 92.

CONNECTING FABRIC—Murtagh, William J. *Keeping Time*, p. 93-94.

Goldberger, Paul. *Buildings Against Cities*, p.9.

MEANING—Norberg-Schulz, Christian. *Genius Loci: Towards a Phenomenology of Architecture.* New York: Rizzoli, 1979, p. 166.

CELEBRATING COMMUNITY— Fleming, Ronald Lee, and Renata von Tscharner. *Place Makers: Public Art that Tells You Where You Are.* Cambridge, Mass.: Townscape Institute; New York: Hastings House, 1981, p. 18.

Bibliography

Alabama Bureau of Tourism & Travel. *100 Dishes to Eat in Alabama Before You Die.* 2005. www.800alabama.com

Alabama Properties Listed on the National Register of Historic Places. Montgomery, Ala.: Alabama Historical Commission, 1998.

Armstrong, Donald E. "Brick Making and the Production of Place at Tuskegee Normal School." *Arris: Journal of the Southeast Chapter of the Society of Architectural Historians* 16 (2005): 28-36.

Ascoli, Peter M. *Julius Rosenwald: The Man Who Built Sears, Roebuck and Advanced the Cause of Black Education in the American South.* Bloomington, Ind.: Indiana University Press, 2006.

Bacon, Edmund N. *Design of Cities.* Rev. ed. 1974. Har-mondsworth, UK: Penguin Books, 1976.

Barkan, Marylon. "Pre-Construction Report: Documentation and Preservation Recommendations for the Lois Jean Delany Opera House, Murphy High School, Mobile, Alabama." Mobile: 1998.

Barnett, Jonathan. *Redesigning Cities: Principles, Practice, Implementation.* Chicago: Planners Press, 2003.

Bennett, Lola. "Historic American Engineering Record: Swann Bridge (Joy Bridge)." HAER No. AL-201, 2003.

Billmeier, Katherine Estes, Philip A. Morris, and J. Scott

Howell, eds. *Vulcan & Vulcan Park: Celebrating 100 Years of Birmingham's Colossal Icon.* Birmingham, Ala.: Vulcan Park Foundation, 2004.

Blount County Historical Society. *The Heritage of Blount County.* Blountsville, Ala.: Blount County Historical Society, 1972.

Bowsher, Alice Meriwether. *Alabama Architecture: Looking at Building and Place.* Tuscaloosa, Ala.: University of Alabama Press, 2001.

Bridges, Edwin C. "Lafayette in Alabama." Paper for The Thirteen, Nov. 2, 2000.

Brooks, Daniel Fate. "Wilcox Female Institute: A Monument to the Past." *Perpetual Harvest* [a MacMillan Bloedel regional newsletter, Pine Hill, Ala., ca. 1978-82].

Bunnell, Gene. *Making Places Special: Stories of Real Places Made Better by Planning.* Chicago: Planners Press, 2003.

Clay County Courthouse Centennial, 1906-2006, Ashland, Alabama: Official Souvenir Program, 2006.

Damle, Hemant S. "Historic American Buildings Survey: Rickwood Field." HABS No. AL-897, 1993.

Davis, Christopher. "The Dwight Textile Mill of Alabama City, Alabama: A Case Study of Welfare Capitalism." Research paper, Samford University, 2003. http://www. samford.edu/schools/artsci/scs/wdavis.html

Dean, Andrea Oppenheimer. "Keeping the Spirit Alive by Moving Ahead." *Architectural Record* 194, no. 3 (March 2006), 76, 78.

Ehrenhalt, Alan. "The Empty Square." *Preservation* 52, no. 2 (March-April 2000). 42-51.

Ellison, Rhoda Coleman. *History of Huntingdon College, 1854-1954.* Tuscaloosa, Ala.: University of Alabama Press, 1954.

Embree, Edwin R. *Julius Rosenwald Fund: A Review to June 30, 1929.* Chicago: The Fund, 1929.

"Eufaula Carnegie Library: Celebrating 100 Years, 1904-2004." Pamphlet, n.d.

The Faith of Jason Malbis. Daphne, Ala.: Malbis Plantation, 1967.

Fleming, John, Hugh Honour, and Nikolaus Pevsner. *Penguin Dictionary of Architecture and Landscape Architecture.* Harmondsworth, Middlesex, England: Penguin Books, 1998.

Fleming, Ronald Lee, and Renata von Tscharner. *Place Makers: Public Art that Tells You Where You Are.* Cambridge, Mass.: Townscape Institute; New York: Hastings House, 1981.

Florida, Richard. *The Rise of the Creative Class, and How It's Transforming Work, Leisure, Community and Everyday Life.* New York: Basic Books, 2002.

French, Roderick S. "On Preserving America: Some Philosophical Observations." In *Preservation: Toward an Ethic in the 1980s,* 182-92. Washington, D.C.: National Trust for Historic Preservation, 1980.

Gamble, Robert S. *The Alabama Catalog: Historic American Buildings Survey, A Guide to the Early Architecture of the State.* Tuscaloosa, Ala.: University of Alabama Press, 1987.

Glassie, Henry. *Vernacular Architecture.* Bloomington, Ind.: Indiana University Press, 2000.

Goldberger, Paul. *Buildings Against Cities: The Struggle to Make Places.* Birmingham, Ala.: Birmingham Historical Society and Harbert Corporation, 1989.

Goodman, Paul, and Percival Goodman. *Communitas: Means of Livelihood and Ways of Life.* 2nd ed. rev. New York: Random House, Vintage Books, 1960.

Gould, Elizabeth Barrett. *From Fort to Port: An Architectural History of Mobile, Alabama, 1711-1918.* Tuscaloosa, Ala.: University of Alabama Press, 1988.

Graham, Patterson Toby. *A Right to Read: Segregation and Civil Rights in Alabama's Public Libraries, 1900-1965.* Tuscaloosa, Ala.: University of Alabama Press, 2002.

Greene County Historical Society. *A Goodly Heritage: Memories of Greene County.* Edited by Mary Morgan Glass. Eutaw, Ala.: Greene County Historical Society, 1977.

The Heritage of Blount County, Alabama. Clanton, Ala.: Heritage Publishing Consultants, 1999.

Helms, Julian. "Edmund Pettus still bridging gaps." *The Selma Times-Journal* (Feb. 25, 2006).

Historic American Buildings Survey/Historic American Engineering Record (HABS/HAER). "Built in America: Historic American Buildings Survey/Historic American Engineering Record, 1933-Present." http://memory.loc.gov/ammem/collections/habs_haer/index.html

Historic Mooresville: A Guide to the First Town Incorporated by the Alabama Territorial Legislature. Mooresville, Ala.: Town of Mooresville, 2001.

Hoffschwelle, Mary S. *The Rosenwald Schools of the American South.* Gainesville, Fla.: University Press of Florida, 2006.

Hughes, Delos D. "A Kentucky Builder in the New South: The M. T. Lewman and Falls City Construction Companies in Alabama, 1897-1915." *The Alabama Review* 59, no. 2 (April 2006): 107-42.

Jacobs, Jane. *The Death and Life of Great American Cities.* New York: Random House, Vintage Books, 1961.

Jolly, Tes Randle. "Dollarhide Days: Famous Southern Deer Camp Carries on Old Traditions." *Deer & Deer Hunting* 28, no.8 (June 2005): 29-32.

Jones, Jerry B. "History of Nichols Memorial Library." http://www.rootsweb.com/~alneags/indexlibword.html

Keys, Anita. "Picture L.A.: Landmarks of a New Generation." *Conservation at the Getty* newsletter 9.2 (Summer 1994). http://getty.edu/conservation/publications/newsletters/9_2/picture.html

Kierstead, Matthew. "Historic American Engineering Record: Vulcan Statue and Park." HAER No. AL-29, 1993.

Krier, Rob. *Urban Space.* New York: Rizzoli, 1979.

Lancaster, Clay. *Eutaw: The Builders and Architecture of an Ante-Bellum Southern Town.* Eutaw, Ala.: Greene County Historical Society, 1979.

Lynch, Kevin. *Good City Form.* Cambridge, Mass.: MIT Press, 1981.

_____. *The Image of the City.* Cambridge, Mass.: MIT Press, 1960.

Malbis Memorial Church. Athens: Ekdotike Hellados, n.d.

McCluskey, Sybil Talley. "Howard Gardner Nichols and Dwight Manufacturing Company." *Northeast Alabama Settlers* 31, no. 4 (April 1993). http://www.rootsweb.com/~alneags/indexnewnichol.html

McLin, Elva Bell. *Athens State College: A Definitive History, 1821-1991.* Athens, Ala.: Athens State College Foundation, 1991.

McQueen, John D. *A Factual History of "Dollarhide" With Some Sidelights and Observations.* Privately published: ca. 1945.

Morris, Philip A. *Vulcan and His Times.* Birmingham, Ala.: Birmingham Historical Society, 1995.

Mumford, Lewis. *The City in History: Its Origins, Its Transformations, and Its Prospects.* New York: Harcourt, Brace & World, 1961.

Murtagh, William J. "Aesthetic and Social Dimensions of Historic Districts." In *Historic Districts: Identification, Social Aspects and Preservation,* 9-16. Washington, DC: National Trust for Historic Preservation, 1975.

_____. "Historic Preservation and Urban Neighborhoods." *Monumentum* 13 (1976): 62-69.

_____. *Keeping Time: The History and Theory of Preservation in America.* 3rd ed. Hoboken, N. J.: John Wiley & Sons, 2006.

Muschamp, Herbert. "The Secret History of 2 Columbus Circle." *The New York Times* (Jan. 8, 2006).

National Park Service. "Carnegie Libraries: The Future Made Bright." Teaching with Historic Places Lesson Plans. http://www.cr.nps.gov/nr/twhp/wwwlps/lessons/50carnegie/50carnegie.htm

_____. *Russell Cave: Russell Cave National Monument, Alabama.* Washington, D.C.: U. S. Government Printing Office, 1999, reprint.

_____. *Selma to Montgomery: National Historic Trail, Alabama.* Washington, D.C.: U. S. Government Printing Office, 2005.

_____. *Tuskegee Institute: National Historic Site, Alabama.* Washington, D.C.: U. S. Government Printing Office, 1979, reprint.

National Register of Historic Places nominations of individual properties and districts. On file, Alabama Historical Commission.

"New Deal Art in Alabama Post Offices and Federal Buildings." *Alabama Arts: Public Art Trails in Alabama 2005* 21, no. 2 (2005): 42-43.

Norberg-Schulz, Christian. *Genius Loci: Towards a Phenomenology of Architecture.* New York: Rizzoli, 1979.

Owen, Marie Bankhead. *The Story of Alabama: A History of the State.* 5 vols. New York: Lewis Historical Publishing Co., 1949.

Panhorst, Michael W. "Confederate Monument Alabama State Capitol. Historic Structure Report: Statement of Historical Significance." McKay Lodge, Inc., 2002.

Project for Public Spaces (PPS). http://www.pps.org

Rogers, William Warren, Robert David Ward, Leah Rawls Atkins, and Wayne Flynt. *Alabama: The History of a Deep South State.* Tuscaloosa, Ala.: University of Alabama Press, 1994.

Roth, Leland M. *Understanding Architecture: Its Elements, History, and Meaning.* Boulder, Colo.: Westview Press, 1993.

Rybczynski, Witold. "The New Downtowns." *The Atlantic Monthly* 271 (May 1993): 98-106.

Saylor, Henry H. *Dictionary of Architecture.* New York: John Wiley & Sons, 1952.

Scott, John B., Jr. "Paint Rock Valley." *Alabama Heritage* 52 (Spring 1999): 32-42.

Sharp, Greta. "A Source of Life, A Source of Faith, A Source of Hope." *Spring Hill Alumni Magazine* (Summer/Fall 2004), 31-33.

Shelby, Thomas Mark. "From Beaux-Arts to Modernism: The Alabama Architecture of D. O. Whilldin, 1881-1970." Master's thesis, University of Alabama, Tuscaloosa, Ala., 2006.

Smith, Winston. *The People's City: The Glory and the Grief of an Alabama Town, 1850-1874.* Demopolis, Ala.: Marengo County Historical Society, 2003.

Southern Poverty Law Center. *The Civil Rights Memorial.* Pamphlet, n.d.

_____. "Maya Lin, Memorial Designer." http://www.splcenter.org/crm/lin.jsp

Special Committee on Historic Preservation, United States Conference of Mayors. Albert Rains and Laurance G. Henderson, eds. *With Heritage So Rich.* New York: Random House, 1966.

Thornton, J. Mills III. *Dividing Lines: Municipal Politics and the Struggle for Civil Rights in Montgomery, Birmingham, and Selma.* Tuscaloosa, Ala.: University of Alabama Press, 2002.

Van Pelt, Robert Jan and Carroll William Westfall. *Architectural Principles in the Age of Historicism.* New Haven, Conn.: Yale University Press, 1991.

Weiss, Ellen. "Robert R. Taylor of Tuskegee: An Early Black American Architect. *Arris: Journal of the Southeast Chapter of the Society of Architectural Historians* 2 (1991): 3-19.

_____. "Tuskegee." Handout prepared for Sept. 29, 2006, tour during the annual meeting of SESAH (Southeast Chapter of the Society of Architectural Historians).

Whyte, William H. *City: Rediscovering the Center.* New York: Anchor Books / Doubleday, 1988.

Your State Coliseum. Booklet for the open house and dedication, October 1953.

INDEX

ABOUT THE AUTHOR

ALICE MERIWETHER BOWSHER is an architectural historian and preservationist whose books include *Alabama Architecture: Looking at Building and Place, Design Review in Historic Districts, House Detective,* and *Town Within a City.* She serves as Alabama Advisor to the National Trust for Historic Preservation.

ABOUT THE PHOTOGRAPHER

M. LEWIS KENNEDY, JR., is a commercial photographer specializing in creating images of the built environment. His work has appeared in trade magazines and a variety of general publications, most notably *Alabama Architecture: Looking at Building and Place.*

ABOUT THE ALABAMA ARCHITECTURAL FOUNDATION

The ALABAMA ARCHITECTURAL FOUNDATION is a nonprofit organization which seeks to heighten the public's appreciation and understanding of architecture and to promote good design within Alabama communities. Proceeds from this book will be used to provide scholarships and loans to deserving students pursuing an education in architecture or related design disciplines. Charles A. Moss, Jr., AIA, is Executive Director.